C

Robert N

of

westminster pre.

D1110457

strengths

ol. 2

1984

248.4
R6462

49125

WILLIAM B. EERDMANS PUBLISHING COMPANY
GRAND RAPIDS, MICHIGAN

❋ *Spirituality and Human Emotion* ❋

By ROBERT C. ROBERTS

Library of Congress Cataloging in Publication Data

Roberts, Robert Campbell, 1942–
  Spirituality and human emotion.

  Bibliography: p. 133
  1. Christian Life — 1960– . 2. Emotions.
I. Title.
BV4501.2.R614   1982   248.4   82-13774
ISBN 0-8028-1939-7

Contents

Preface   vii

Chapter 1   Introduction   1
        2   Emotion and the Fruit of the Spirit   12
        3   Something Eternal in the Self   25
        4   The Death of Ivan Ilych   39
        5   Humility as a Moral Project   57
        6   Gratitude   74
        7   Hope   91
        8   Compassion   109

List of Works Cited   133

Preface

IN the preface to *The Sickness Unto Death* Kierkegaard's persona, Anti-Climacus, warns that "to many the form of this 'exposition' will perhaps seem strange; it will seem to them too strict to be edifying, and too edifying to be strictly scientific" (142). He goes on to say that he would consider it a fault for his book to be too strict to be edifying, though no doubt, because of its strictness, some people are not up to being edified by it. (As to whether it is too edifying to be strictly scientific, he claims to have no opinion.) But such a book requires a rather special reader, one who combines a certain ability to think with a desire to become something more than an intellectual master of Christianity.

The present book makes similar demands. It is neither for people who think that rigor in religious studies entails "the neutral scientific standpoint" (whatever that is) nor for people who want to be edified without being educated. I am a philosophy teacher by trade, and a Christian by profession. My taste runs to clarity and distinctions, but because I am a Christian I have little interest in analyses of Christianity which contribute nothing to people's growth in the faith. In this book I have tried to keep the philosophic niceties within the bounds of spiritual usefulness.

This book is for people who like to *reflect* about this bizarre and beautiful business of being human, and one of its claims is that such reflection can be an aid to growth in the life which we live before God. If the book succeeds, I think it would especially please a person who has suffered a certain kind of disappointment. On the one hand she has been disappointed by most of the "spirituality" literature that she finds on the shelves of Christian bookstores. It's a little like a down pillow. If you're sleepy, it may be just what you need; but if you want something to stand on, something to enable a higher reach, it squooshes down too easily. You need something firmer, more resistant. On the other hand, she has perhaps read a bit of academic theology or taken a course in religion at her local university. Here she is disappointed not because of a lack of intellectual firmness, but because what can be reached by standing here is not food for her spirit. The stool is strong enough, but it's in front of the wrong cupboard. If she wanted descriptions of religions, or historical knowledge, or an introduction to the puzzles of the Trinity or hermeneutics, or if she wanted to know about the swarm of hypotheses concerning the origins of the New Testament documents, she would not be disappointed. But she is disappointed: for she has opened a cupboard looking for food, and has found nothing but various tools and games.

If this book succeeds, such a reader will delight in it because it is analytical enough to provide some firm intellectual elevation, and because it locates the stool in front of the cupboard where the food is. To those whose enthusiasm for philosophic niceties does not stop at the bounds of spiritual usefulness but goes nearer to theoretical exhaustiveness (or exhaustion), I offer my apologies.

Let me say a bit about my debts. Søren Kierkegaard's influence is pervasive, especially in the great weight I place on the passions as basic to Christian emotion. But this book should not be taken as an exposition of his thought; he is an inspiration more than a source. I was in conversation with Richard H. Olmsted during much of the writing of the book, and many a chapter bears the mark of his incisive mind. Paul L. Holmer has shaped my thinking in ways beyond my power to reckon; but in particular his preoccupation with the "emotions, passions, and feelings" has served as a constant point of reference and stimulus to reflection over the past dozen or so years since I began to be his student. My wife, Elizabeth Vanderkooy Roberts, read most of the book in various of its stages and made many helpful suggestions.

Most of the book was drafted while I was a fellow at the Institute for Ecumenical and Cultural Research at St. John's University, Collegeville, Minnesota. In the beautiful setting there among the lakes the Reverend Robert Bilheimer, Sr. Dolores Schuh, and Fr. Wilfred Theisen of the Institute made our stay pleasant and carefree; and conversations with the other fellows stimulated the mind and uplifted the spirit. Thanks are due to Western Kentucky University for a sabbatical leave during the academic year 1980-81, and to the Institute for Advanced Christian Studies for a grant which made it possible to extend a one semester sabbatical to two.

Thank you to the *Christian Century* for permission to print, in Chapter 1, a few paragraphs from my essay "Faith and Modern Humanity: Two Approaches." Bible quotations are from the Revised Standard Version. I use a simple, in-text method of referring to quoted sources; full bibliographical information about those sources is to be found at the end of the book.

❋ 1 ❋
Introduction

IN the 1960s a number of American and British writers who styled themselves "theologians" gave voice to a cry of anguish on behalf of Modern Man. The trouble, in a nutshell, was that this recently evolved paragon found himself rather at sea religiously, having outgrown the Christianity of his fathers. Nurtured on science and secularism, he now heard a hollow ring in the cadences of the older theology. Perhaps "anguished" is not quite the word for this cry, for there was in it an adolescent rambunctiousness which signaled the mischievous joy these writers took in their theatrical flash.

The kernel of truth in their thinking is this: the gospel very often seems alien to us. It seems to fit ill our understanding of ourselves and the world. St. Paul's talk about joy and hope and peace in the Lord seems, sometimes, to belong in another world than the one we inhabit. More often than we are comfortable to admit, we find ourselves feeling what those writers in the sixties said we should feel: a twinge of uneasiness at speaking about heaven outside of church; the sense that Jesus' death and resurrection can't really be brought to bear on our daily routine, our social life, our money making, our recreation; an inability to see with the heart the goodness of the Good News; a certain emptiness in our prayers. Our faith lacks the confidence, the clarity, the childlike enthusiasm we seem to find in Christians in other ages of the church.

Whatever else Christianity may be, it is a set of emotions. It is love of God and neighbor, grief about one's own waywardness, joy in the merciful salvation of our God, gratitude, hope, and peace. So if I don't love God and my neighbor, abhor my sins, and rejoice in my redemption, if I am not grateful, hopeful, and at peace with God and myself, then it follows that I am alienated from Christianity, though I was born and bred in the bosom of the Presbyterian Church, am baptized and confirmed and willing in good conscience to affirm the articles of the Creed.

It is probable that in ages of Christian culture the *sense* of the alienness of the gospel is less than in times and places in which Christians or nominal Christians rub daily against those who deny their faith. Thus in the earliest centuries of Christianity, and in our time since the Enlightenment, one could expect more people to experience the oddness of Christianity than, say, in the Middle Ages. St. Paul was certainly vivid about the impression of foolishness that Christianity made on outsiders, and I suppose that his church members often had the same impression if they had one foot outside the Christian ghetto, as most of us do. If people in the Middle Ages felt less alien from Christianity than people in the first and twentieth centuries, maybe this is less a tribute to their faith than a symptom of a culture-engendered blindness.

But since you and I are evidently Modern People, and since the cry of anguish has been uttered on our behalf, let us consider the problem of alienation from Christianity in this age. In the remainder of this chapter I shall set forth two approaches to the problem of modern unbelief. Each possesses its own diagnosis and corresponding prescription for a cure. The first approach is very widely taken, both unselfconsciously by preachers and other religious teachers, and self-consciously by professional theologians. I shall take Rudolf Bultmann as a typical practitioner of this method, because he is so forthright in his account of it. The other approach, strongly contrasting with Bultmann's, is embodied in the writings of Søren Kierkegaard, to whom I am deeply indebted for many of the ideas in this book. But Kierkegaard is not really charting territory all his own in ministering to our alienation from Christianity. He is only a very adept practitioner of a prescription which has been found in all ages of the church. Bultmann's approach I shall call the "reinterpretation" approach; Kierkegaard's I name the "therapy" approach.

BULTMANN traces our uneasiness with New Testament Christianity to a fundamental flaw in the New Testament: the message is expressed in a "language" which is not that of modern people and which, moreover, is basically incoherent. What language is this? If you thought it was ancient Greek or Hebrew, you were wrong. True, these are not widely known among modern people, but this difficulty is easily avoided by the use of scholarly translations. But the "language" in which the New Testament is couched doesn't go away so easily; Matthew and Romans use it even after they've been put into English. The "language" Bultmann is talking about is called "Mythology." According to Bultmann, it is because Paul spoke and wrote this language, so foreign to our modern mind, that we today do not understand him and are unable to put his message into practice in our lives.

What is the vocabulary of Mythology, and what meaning was it able to convey? Let us begin with the second question. Roughly, Bultmann describes an experience like this:

Our lives are given a sort of dull, everyday meaning by established patterns of activity, and by the "values" which lie behind these activities. We work and play, compete with others for money and prestige, enjoy our daily pleasures and avoid pains whenever possible, rear our children, and plan for the future (carefully guarding against thinking too clearly about what it inevitably holds for us — decline and death). But extreme situations are sometimes so disruptive that the entire meaning structure of a person's life can be called into question. I was a student when National Guard troops shot and killed students on the campus of Kent State University. I remember vividly the attitude caused in some, at least momentarily, by that event. They were already opposed to the Establishment's conduct of the Vietnam War, but most of them still had plenty at stake in the American way of life: it provided them with comforts, potential careers, values, and ways of understanding themselves, which they were far from ready to abandon.

But when the news broke that this Establishment had actually killed some of their fellow students, it was as though the whole system of values and expectations associated with their personal history as Americans was shattered, as though their past had fallen away, leaving them suspended in value-space, without the security of an "orientation." They also found, however, that this shattering of life's old meaning was a cloud with a silver lining. As they sometimes put it, they had been "radicalized." Precisely in the death of the old self and its values, they found a freedom for ethical activities and a resigned acceptance of whatever the future might hold for them — freedom and acceptance not possible for a person clinging desperately to his or her "past."

What has such an experience to do with Christianity? Bultmann seems to believe that the disciples had an experience like this when they beheld, hanging upon the cross, the man in whom all their hopes had recently come to rest. In his death they experienced the shattering of their world; but at the same time they experienced a new freedom so radical that they came to speak of being given "new life" and becoming a "new creation." This experience, then, is the *meaning* of the language of Mythology, according to Bultmann.

And now, what about its *vocabulary*? If the biblical writers had told the story the way I just did, and stuck with metaphors like "new creation," we would have no difficulty in understanding them—nor, perhaps, in gaining a freedom like that of the disciples when we confront the message that their experience revealed to them. Unfortunately they did not rely only on metaphors to express their new self-understanding: instead, according to Bultmann, they spoke as persons of their time were bound to speak of such matters: they spoke Mythology. To express the experience of inward liberation they had had in facing up to the cross of Jesus, they said, "Jesus was raised from the dead, and sits at the right hand of God the Father"; they said, "God was in Christ reconciling the world to himself"; they said, "Jesus is the Son of God"; "Jesus died for your sins."

Now these statements seem to be about who Jesus is, or what he did, or what happened to him, or where he is. But in Bultmann's view, they are not really about such things. They are examples of the strange vocabulary of Mythology; they are a way (and indeed a very misleading way) of speaking about that experience of freedom which the disciples had when their master was crucified, and which modern people can have too. For ancient people, evidently this was a natural way of speaking.

But, says Bultman, modern people hear these sentences very differently. It does not easily occur to us that this may be a way of speaking of one's self-understanding. Rather, we immediately jump to the conclusion that when Paul, for example, says "Jesus was raised from the dead," this must be a statement *about Jesus*. And so we puzzle over such statements, and find them quite incredible and eccentric, or if we are very befuddled we may even believe them (whatever that might mean). But in any case we fail completely to understand them, because the form of expression is so exceedingly odd. Since we have no clue that the words describe the experience of radical freedom, they are utterly useless in helping us to have that experience.

The fault lies with the New Testament, which hides its own light under the bushel of a malformed language. And so, if we moderns are to share in the blessings of which the New Testament speaks, we need the help of someone who understands the language of Mythology and can translate it into a language with which the modern world is familiar. We need a helper who can tell us the *real* meaning of expressions like "Jesus Christ," "resurrection," "God," "heaven," and "creation."

That helper is, of course, Rudolf Bultmann himself, along with all the other demythologizers of our time. So the cure for the modern person's uneasiness with Christianity is a special technique, an operation to be performed by professionals on the language of the New Testament.

BULTMANN is a paradigm of the reinterpreting approach to reconciling Modern Man with Christianity. What he does in his writings is something we can see happening in a much less formal and systematic way in pulpits across the land. The method is to find some generally available experience or insight, some widely acceptable "meaning" that can pass for a religious experience or insight, and then to claim that this is what the gospel (or some text) is *really* about. Preachers often attempt this method so haphazardly and shabbily that if anybody thought for a moment (and the preacher trusts that no one will), he would immediately realize that the preacher's meaning couldn't possibly be the meaning of the text, and that if it is, there's no explaining why people have taken the Bible so seriously all these years. The "meaning" of some passage from Ephesians or the Gospel of John is often reduced to a piece of proverbial wisdom which anybody over the age of eight could easily have thought up without the help of any text. In fact, the preacher's ingenuity resides not in finding the thought, but in making it seem plausible that it was derived from the text. Only slightly better is the preacher who gets her biblical "meanings" out of rational be-

havior therapy and has enough of a philosophy of life that one
can detect a strand of consistency from Sunday to Sunday.

The theologian who takes the reinterpreting approach generally has a more critical audience than the preacher and so has
to come up with a "meaning" that can plausibly be thought to
be religious. As is well known, Bultmann imports his "meaning"
from existentialism, in particular the early writing of Martin
Heidegger. Other theologians get their "meanings" from depth
psychology (in particular from C.G. Jung), from the process philosophy of Alfred North Whitehead, from German idealism,
from an inspirational interpretation of evolution, from common
sense morality with or without a divine tinge, from Eastern or
Western mysticism, from Ludwig Wittgenstein's philosophy, from
Marxist social theory, and so forth. But these "theologies" are
all only permutations on the strategy exemplified in Bultmann.
The assumption is that the Bible and the orthodox Christian
tradition as it stands are not fit nourishment for humanity come
of age. And so the texts and the language of faith need to be
energized, injected with some spiritual nutrient from non-Christian sources, brought up to a caloric content sufficient to the
fires of our modern spiritual metabolism. Presumably Whitehead's philosophy, existentialism, and Marxism are more easily
chewed and digested than the doctrines of God, sin, and atonement deriving from Jesus, Paul, Augustine, and Luther. But since,
for one reason or another, we want to feel we are still within
the Christian tradition, we retain the shell language, the words
and phrases of Christianity, while exchanging the concepts they
once expressed for the more digestible modern ones.

This approach is appealing for at least three reasons. First,
the compliments here all go to Modern Man who, scientific and
come of age, has outgrown Christianity—who looks back on it
the way an adult looks back on the antics of his youth, with a
disowning smile of condescension. It's a pat on the back for the
brave grown-ups. Second, it confirms our resistance to the au-
thority and transcendence of God. Christianity has always claimed
that God is sovereign and speaks in his own good time and way,
which may not always sound sweetly in the ears of sinners. Since
we would like God to speak to us according to our schedules
and in ways which seem reasonable and worthy of God and
ourselves, this is a painful aspect of Christianity. We don't take

naturally to the teachings about sin and atonement, about the unique incarnation of God in Jesus, and about the cross. So when theologians come along and tell us that our discomforts here are due to our having outgrown these teachings, we resonate to the account. Third, this approach is appealing because it makes spiritual renewal primarily the responsibility of the intellectuals who concoct and administer the injections of modern spiritual material into the Christian tradition. The job is one for professionals—theologians and preachers and maybe a poet here and there—instead of a task set for each individual in the inwardness of his own heart and the outwardness of a daily life of loving action. The emphasis is no longer on the hard task of purging a sinful life of those elements which stand between it and God, and of growing up by letting one's mind be painfully (but also joyfully) remade and one's nature transformed by the grace of God in Jesus Christ. The emphasis now is upon "the task of hermeneutics."

I want now to contrast the avenue of reinterpretation with the therapeutic approach to our alienation from Christianity. Instead of assuming that people really ought to resonate immediately to Christianity, we start with the observation that Christianity is and always was a strange doctrine. Instead of being surprised that people do not understand it or that they do not profess it without undergoing an alteration of character, we note that Christianity contains some opaque and offensive elements and implies a mental and behavioral life which is bound to seem alien to almost everybody. From this point of view what is alarming is not that the majority feel alienated from Christianity; it should be alarming if people seem to be assimilating it too easily and en masse, somewhat in the way they assimilate patriotism. That is cause for the alarm that what they are taking in is not quite Christianity.

The Christian explanation of the strangeness of Christianity has, broadly, two parts: first, God's ways are not our ways and he is not bound to adapt himself completely to our ways; second, we are sinners who consequently have a perverted outlook on God and ourselves. Some people may think these two parts of the explanation reduce to one: the difference between God's ways and ours *is* our sinfulness. But I doubt that this is true; at any rate, it certainly need not be. God's ways might be surprising and strange to us even if we weren't sinners; but I do think that if we weren't sinners we would more gladly bow to his strange ways, and would get used to them more quickly than we do.

This approach suggests that to overcome our alienation from Christianity we need to alter not Christianity, but *ourselves*. Kierkegaard traces our uneasiness with New Testament Christianity not to any deficiency in the New Testament or the traditional theology, but to a malformation of the hearts of modern people. We do not need a new "meaning" for the language of faith, but a reordering of our passions and attitudes such that we will have a use in our life for the beliefs of Christianity and the language of faith. The trouble with many of us is that the deepest motives of our lives are not sufficiently congruent with the demands and blessings of the gospel for it to find a welcome place in our hearts.

Since the psychological barriers to faith take many forms, differing from individual to individual and from age to age, Christianity is in perpetual need of reflective diagnosticians and resourceful strategists for "reintroducing Christianity" (to borrow a phrase from Kierkegaard). Their purpose will be to stimulate and guide people to reflect deeply about what it is to be human and to struggle with themselves in such a way that the Christian teachings will begin to make sense for them. The task will be to suggest disciplines by which people can grow. It will be to head off debilitating confusions engendered by the prevailing mental culture. It will be to warn against the perennial pitfalls of the spiritual life, to guide along the narrow path of righteousness. In other words, the task will be to find ways of curing people of their insensitivity to Christianity—and this amounts to helping them come into a passionate relationship with God.

Of course this is nothing that Kierkegaard invented. Pastors have been up to this sort of thing as long as Christianity has existed. It is interesting that we even have built into our language the suggestion that the Christian leader is involved in a therapeutic task. For in some traditions the pastor is called a curate (in French *curé*). His task is to care for his people as a doctor cares for his patients, assuming disease or at least the threat of illness, and attempting to cure them, or at least to keep them healthy. The pastor cures them of their worldliness, their alienation from God, their disability to relate happily to Jesus Christ. It needs to be said too that just as a doctor doesn't actually cure anybody, but only facilitates the natural healing mechanisms of the body, so the pastor does not himself cure anybody, but only facilitates the cure that God alone can effect.

It goes without saying, I suppose, that if we conceive the task thus, there is no way to cure Modern Man of his impotence to appropriate Christian teachings. If Bultmann's approach is correct, then it is just possible that some theologian in her study might cure the entire age in one fell swoop. (Bultmann himself pictures a whole generation of busy theologians accomplishing this.) The theologian would only have to find some "meaning" which the whole age is able to assimilate, inject the language of faith with it, and send out a bulletin to all the pastors. Once Modern Man caught on that Christianity no longer "meant" that dark and foolish stuff, but now "meant" something clear and obviously important, he would flock into the churches and feed hungrily on the Word. But if we have qualms about changing Christianity into something other than itself to make it palatable to people, and if we lay the blame for its tastelessness not on the Bread of Life but on the palates of the people to whom it is offered, then the task will have to be one of laboriously curing each individual palate of its infirmity. If Christian leaders think of themselves as curates, they will not try to cure Modern Man, but will address themselves to modern men and women, individual sufferers who have varying difficulties with Christianity and who must be led each along his or her path of personal growth.

W HY do persons of goodwill toward Christianity, church-goers and seekers of God, so often not *feel* like Christians? The personal impediments are numerous and various, but we can put them in three categories. We can distinguish distresses that are peculiar to individuals, those that are peculiar to an age or intellectual environment or social group, and those that are generically human.

One person, for example, may have been taught a perverted concept of God through early childhood training: she may be so in the grip of the idea that God is like a finicky, legalistic, and manipulative bachelor uncle that she cannot hear the good news of the gospel. Such highly individualized hindrances are nearly impossible to itemize, and call for the ingenuity of the pastor or even the Christian psychiatrist.

Other ills are more the special product of a broad intellectual environment. Several of C. S. Lewis's writings are addressed to widely felt impediments bred by the spirit of the modern age. His book *Miracles*, for example, is aimed at dispelling a general view of reality which he calls naturalism. *The Abolition of Man* is an effort to raise people's consciousness of some ideas, generally diffused in our culture, about the status of "values" and the nature of the human self. It seems almost in our blood to consider "values" trivial and subjective as compared with "facts," and he calls us back to the ancient and solid view that "values" have a universal and objective character. The trivializing of "values" makes truncated people with intellects and instincts, but no hearts; and Lewis argues, warming the cockles of *my* heart, for the heartiness of man. In a little address entitled "Modern Theology and Biblical Criticism" he debunks, in a few deft strokes, the kind of literary observations and historical reconstructions which tend to call into question the historical basis of the Christian faith.

Kierkegaard also engaged in reflective antienvironment therapy on behalf of Christian faith. He called attention to the Hegelian reinterpretation of Christianity which was influential in his day, and especially to the tendency to "naturalize" Jesus Christ, to make him over into something quite commodious to our common sense and our worldly ways of thinking. With stinging irony and a gripping wit he also threw light on the spiritually deadening effect of the modern tendency to turn all conceptual material (including Christian teaching and ethics) into grist for lectures and university courses. The present chapter is another attempt to alert Christian seekers to the impediments which hang in the intellectual air; if you see the reinterpreting approach to Christian spirituality for what it is, you will be less likely to be derailed by it. Forewarned is forearmed.

But a less polemical kind of nurturing reflection is also important. In every age, people have a tendency to trivialize human life, to fail to appreciate the momentousness, the glory, of being human; this is the third category of impediments. And so the

Christian therapist has the job of reminding us, in gripping ways, that we are not just very smart animals, but that there is, as Kierkegaard put it, "something eternal" in us—features of us which are definitely Godward. If we can appreciate *that* in a heartfelt way, then the message that God is our Father can begin to take emotional root in us. Something similar can be said about guilt. Guilt, in the Christian context, does not mean that one feels like a worm. It is, if I may speak a little perversely, a noble thing, a consequence of being a responsible person before God. That we are guilty is an aspect of the momentousness of being a self. Horses and dogs, and even chimpanzees, can't be guilty, because they can't stand responsibly before God. Kierkegaard thought long and hard about the momentousness of being human, often focusing his reflections around the emotions of despair, anxiety, and guilt. And we will do the same as our discussion progresses.

This book is an exercise in therapeutic Christian reflection. Most of it is aimed at the third of the three types of impediments I have distinguished above. It is mostly nonpolemical and considers the general human condition rather than idiosyncratic spiritual ills. In the next chapter I shall discuss human emotion, claiming that emotions are ways of "seeing" ourselves and our world that grow out of concerns of one sort or another. Since as Christians we are very much interested in the formation of some emotions and the eradication of others, I shall attempt to say some things about how and to what extent our emotions are within our control. The Christian emotions, then, are ways of "seeing" which are determined by the peculiar Christian concepts and the scheme of beliefs which give rise to those concepts. But all emotions are based on some concern or other, and the fruits of the Spirit such as hope and peace and gratitude are no different from other emotions in this respect. No one who lacks the concern which is basic to these emotions will ever have them. So I devote Chapters Three through Five to an analysis and discussion of the concern—indeed, when it is mature, it is a full-blown passion—for the kingdom of God. Negatively described, this passion is the desire to live free from the twin evils of sin and death. Then in the last three chapters I expound three selected fruits of the Holy Spirit: gratitude, hope, and compassion.

❋ 2 ❋
Emotion and the Fruit of the Spirit

AMONG the virtues which constitute the mature Christian life, there are a number which are emotions: gratitude, hope, peace, joy, contrition, and compassion, to name a few. Other virtues, such as patience, perseverance, and self-control, are pretty clearly not emotions (perhaps they could be called "strengths"); and love (whether of God or neighbor) is probably best thought of as a hybrid between emotion and passion (I will have more to say about this distinction momentarily). The emotions, however, are central among those Christian personality characteristics which St. Paul categorizes as the "fruit of the Holy Spirit," and it is on them that I intend to focus.

People who are inclined, as I am, to connect spiritual growth with reflection may be put off by the idea of the fruits of the Holy Spirit for two reasons. First, if these emotions occur simply as a result of God's direct action—when God "takes possession" of an individual's personality—it seems there isn't anything to be *done* to foster them. They are supernatural, and if we covet them, we just have to wait, knowing that God will act. And second, emotions as such (quite apart from any consideration of the supernatural) may seem to be intellectually disreputable. Instead of being the sort of thing you can foster through reflection, they may seem to be something which, like superstition and bad logic, disappears from a person's life as he becomes more reflective. Let me begin by answering these two objections.

In the New Testament, the working of the Holy Spirit is normally not something which occurs under just any conditions; it occurs typically in connection with the preaching of the good news about God's redemption of sinners through the life, death, and resurrection of Jesus of Nazareth. This good news is seen as having a double role: it is the *news* that God has reconciled the world to himself (that is, information about what God has accomplished in Christ), and at the same time an *instrument* by which that reconciliation is worked out, in some small and anticipatory way, in the communities and individuals who give ear to it. The outworking of that reconciliation takes form in people becoming obedient, grateful, hopeful, at peace with themselves and God and their neighbor, and being "filled" with joy in the Lord and love for their brothers and sisters. So great is the role of preaching and hearing the gospel in effecting this transformation, that we could call these fruits "fruits of the gospel." But if we did, they would be no less fruits of the Spirit of God. For the work of reconciliation in which they participate is *God's* work in his people; the gospel is his instrument in this work.

But if this is what the fruits of the Holy Spirit are, and this the way he bears his fruit, then reflection takes on an obvious importance. First, the gospel, being news, is something that can be thought about, meditated on; indeed, it is hard to see how it can be planted in people so as to bear its fruit if it is not in *some* sense thought about or meditated on. We will be doing some such thinking in the course of this book. But beyond a plain meditation on the gospel, the individual interested in deepening his spirituality may find it helpful to become clearer about what emotions are and what kind of control we have over them. The emotions which make up the Christian life are not inscrutable psychological phenomena mysteriously caused by God, as inaccessible to our understanding as the origin of the universe. They are, after all, *emotions*, and since they are, reflection about the nature of emotion may lead to a kind of self-knowledge which can be applied, in various ways, to the task of becoming a Christian. That, at least, is the hope and project of this chapter. The application of these general insights about emotion to the more specific issues of Christian spirituality will be the task of the rest of this book.

But what about our second objection? Aren't emotions, as such, pretty disreputable little items in the panoply of humanalia? Aren't they more like warts than like hands and fingers and toes, at best useless and at worst troublesome little accretions to the personality?

Certainly, when we describe someone as "an emotional type," we do not intend the epithet as a compliment. We mean that he is not quite in possession of himself. He is weak, immature, hollow, shallow, flabby, not "together." Trivial successes and modest beauties, which would only disrupt a stronger man's hairdo, are to him a gale of ecstasy, which "blows him away." He cries easily, even on occasions which only by a stretch of the melodramatic imagination might be thought possibly to warrant a tear. He is useless in times of crisis, being discombobulated by circumstances which a more firmly drawn personality takes in stride.

This is not a pretty picture, and it has led many to be suspicious of emotions in general, and to think that personal maturity is largely a matter of suppressing, if not eradicating, the emotions. But only a little common observation is needed to see the falseness of this picture. The capacity to be affected emotionally is not only a characteristic of weak people but also of very strong ones. Churchill, Socrates, and the apostle Paul were all strong people of deep feeling. As I shall argue in a moment, emotion is founded upon *concerns.* It is the fact, among other things, that they are "driven" by some passion or other—whether it be love of country, concern for intellectual and moral integrity, or the love of God—that makes concerned people such strong, integrated persons. But their passion is also the basis for a wide repertoire of emotions.

The "emotional person" is weak not because he has emotions, but because he has such poor ones, or such a limited repertoire of them. He lacks personal integration and depth not because he feels strongly, but because his feelings are erratic and chaotic, or because he feels strongly about the wrong things, or because he lacks something that ought to be present in addition to his strong feelings, something we might call "presence of mind," "self-possession," or "self-control." And such self-possession may itself be largely a matter of having certain concerns. Most people feel fear when they are endangered, but some "fall apart" and become unable to act intelligently, while others "keep their cool." What might the difference between these types of people be? One kind of difference is this: fear disconcerts some people because they lack a sufficiently strong countervailing concern. For example, part of Socrates' ability to face death with equanimity was that he feared something else (namely the betrayal of his moral self) even more. And a parent may master his fear and go into a burning house largely because he fears something else more than the danger to himself—the death of his children. In such cases the concern for moral integrity or the concern for one's children (which are emotion-dispositions) plays a role in holding the person together.

(It would be wrong to think, as some psychologists do, that countervailing concerns are the *only* explanation of "self-possession." I shall not argue the point here, but I think that the virtues which I called "strengths" at the beginning of this chapter are distinct virtues, and not merely functions of competing concerns. Virtues such as courage, self-control, perseverance, and patience need to be thought of, at least in part, as kinds of *skills*, that is, as skills of psychological self-management. As such these virtues are a kind of self-knowledge, where "knowledge" means not "possession of information" but "possession of know-how.")

An emotion-disposition, as I have already suggested, is always a *concern*. An emotion is a *construal* of one's circumstances (whether that is one's very narrowly immediate circumstances or the "circumstance" that is the whole universe) in a manner relevant to some such concern. Let me illustrate this basic point with a simple example. Consider Hank the gardener and his response to the weatherwoman's prediction of hail. He is apprehensive. Why is Hank apprehensive? Well, because he's got new tomato plants out. But of course this is an incomplete answer, for Hank's having tomato plants out wouldn't explain his apprehensiveness if he didn't *care* about the welfare of those plants. If he were not a conscientious gardener and just did his job because he was paid, perhaps he wouldn't give a flip what happens to the plants. In that case Hank wouldn't be apprehensive about the approaching storm—at least not on account of the tomatoes. So his apprehensiveness is grounded in his concern for his plants. If the storm passes, his apprehensiveness will pass too—most likely into a quietly joyful sense of relief. And this emotion is grounded in the same concern as the other, namely Hank's concern for his tomato plants.

So Hank's concern is what I have called an emotion-disposition. It is not itself an emotion, but instead a *disposition* to a *variety* of emotions. What, then, determines *which* emotion arises in Hank's heart? It is how Hank construes the circumstances which impinge on his concern. If the weatherwoman predicts hail, Hank will see his tomato plants as possibly threatened, and his emotion will be apprehensiveness, fear, anxiety, or some such thing. If the storm passes, then he will construe his plants as safe after all, and he will have a sense of relief; his heart will be glad. If he thinks his plants are being knowingly damaged by a responsible agent (if, say, the teenager next door tears across the tomato patch on his motor bike), his emotion will be anger. If he wakes up on a frosty morning in spring and finds that during the night his neighbor, seeing the danger to Hank's plants, has beneficently covered them while Hank slumbered in oblivion, Hank's emotion will be gratitude. And so forth. So an emotion is a way of "seeing" things, when this "seeing" is grounded in a concern; and a concern is a disposition to have a range of emotions. (Throughout this book I shall for convenience employ the language of vision when I talk about construals [ways of "seeing" things], but of course not all construals are visual. I can construe a person's spoken words as an insult or a compliment, construe the dampness I feel in my baby's pants as the milk she recently sat in, construe the smell of smoke in the house as harmless, etc.)

The application of these ruminations is briefly this. Just as Hank would have no emotional response at all to the news of the approaching storm if he didn't care about anything upon which that news impinges, so the candidate for being a Christian will not respond to the news of the gospel with joy, peace, gratitude, and hope, if she doesn't have the passions upon which *this* news impinges. The gospel message provides people with a distinctive way of construing the world: the maker of the universe is your personal loving Father and has redeemed you from sin and death in the life and death and resurrection of his Son Jesus. You are a child of God, destined along with many brothers and sisters to remain under his protection forever and to be transformed into something unspeakably lovely. Because these others are also his children, you are expected to treat them gently, to help them when they are in need, and in general to respect and love them as fellow heirs of your Father's kingdom. If a person doesn't feel a hunger for the righteousness and eternal life which are proclaimed and promised in the Christian message, then it is not surprising that the gospel falls on "deaf" ears. Those who hunger and thirst for righteousness are the blessed ones, for to them (and them alone) the gospel of Jesus is the satisfaction of peace and joy. Because this concern is an absolute prerequisite to the bearing of spiritual fruit, a large portion of this book is devoted to clarifying what kind of life and consciousness is most likely to give rise to such fruit.

A few pages ago, in connection with Socrates and Churchill and Paul, I spoke of how a certain kind of concern, which I called a passion, can integrate and focus the personality and give a person "character." A passion, then, is a kind of concern, but not every concern is a passion. The word "passion" has a variety of uses in modern English, and I am trading on just one of these. We sometimes speak of a person as "flying into a passion" if he is overcome by a strong emotion. We sometimes say, too, that a person "has a lot of passion," meaning that he is an intense sort of person—that whatever he does he does with gusto. Passion in this sense seems to be largely a genetic endowment. But I am not using the word in either of these two senses. I use it to refer not to emotions, nor to a general spiritedness of personality, but to a person's specific interests, concerns, preoccupations. Thus in the present sense of the word, a person can have a passion for antique automobiles, for justice, for historical scholarship, for the well-being of poor people, for photography, biking, intellectual honesty, or any number of things.

Now I think we would not want to say that Hank the gardener has a passion for those tomato plants of his. He might have a passion for gardening, and even for tomato plants in general, but it would be strange if he had a passion for those particular plants. He is concerned about them, but his concern is not a passion. Why not? The reason, it seems to me, is that his concern for them does not determine sufficiently long stretches of his emotional and active life. He cannot be concerned year in and year out about those plants, in the way that he can be about his children, or biking, or intellectual honesty. That is, his concern for those tomato plants may characterize Hank for a few weeks, but it does not characterize him as a *person*. It is not a character trait.

On the other hand, Socrates' concern for intellectual integrity, the caring for honesty and virtue which led him daily into the marketplace to converse with others and try to get them to care more for virtue than for getting money and fame and preserving their lives—this concern is surely a passion. It forms the deepest regions of his personality. It determines how he daily sees the world and conducts himself, but more than that it gives him a kind of consistency and equanimity in the face of events which would bring others to despair. This points up an ambiguity in our use of the word "character." In one sense everybody, or almost everybody, has character, because everybody has *some* passions. Thus a man's long and steady devotion to money making constitutes his character. But when we say that somebody has character in a second sense, we mean to praise him, to say that he is not easily undone by circumstances—by the disapproval of his colleagues and friends and enemies, by the prospect of losing his position or possessions because of the stand he takes on things. It is Socrates' passion, in part, which makes him a "man of character" in this sense. His passion enables him to remain consistent in his unwillingness to speak any word which he believes untrue or to use any survival tactics which would fit ill with his insistence, throughout his life, on rational discussion and persuasion. But one must not draw a false conclusion here. One might think that only moral passions give a person character in the laudatory sense, but this is not true. One has only to read G. Gordon Liddy's autobiography *Will* to see that a person whose dominant passion is a "will to power" can be a man of character in this sense.

On a less extraordinary level, we meet every day with people whose lives are shaped by deep and abiding concerns. One is possessed with a concern to become famous, another to become rich, yet another to alleviate the sufferings of the poor and hungry. Of course, concerns are often mixed. A woman who deeply desires to become rich may also be interested in fame, and may even have some abiding concern for the hungry. No one, I suppose, has only one single passion. Even a relative saint may not be entirely unconcerned about his reputation, or even his fame. And so it is the *order* of our cares, as Socrates points out, which determines our character. "I tried to persuade each one of you to take care for himself first, and how he could become most good and most wise, before he took care for any of his interests, ... that ... this was the proper order of his care" (from "Apology," Rouse's translation, p. 442). A person with the order of passions that Socrates recommends would qualify as having ethical character. One who had some concern for ethical goodness, but whose concern for it was usually overridden by considerations of fame and pleasure and wealth and safety, would not have (or would have little) ethical character.

And so I think we have here another criterion for distinguishing passions from lesser concerns, though it is certainly not a very precise one. In general, passions are those concerns which, in any given personality, rank higher in the order of the individual's cares. Thus the relative saint I mentioned above would be a person who had a passion for the kingdom of God; that is his overriding concern, the concern by reference to which he attempts to suppress and eradicate competing ones. Even though he still has a concern for fame, he looks upon it with regret or even horror if it goes contrary to his life before God; by virtue of his passion for the kingdom he construes himself as something of a failure, or even as a monstrosity. A person who was not a relative saint would not experience these emotions when contemplating his concern for fame.

Let me summarize. Emotion-dispositions are concerns, and concerns of a special type which can be called passions constitute our character, our inmost self. Passions differ from other concerns in determining a person's actions and emotions over relatively long stretches of his life, and roughly by being "higher" in the order of his cares. If an individual's passions are moral, they give him ethical character. If they are Christian, they give him Christian character. But all passions are emotion-dispositions, and the disposition issues in an emotion when the individual construes his circumstances as impinging upon the object of his passion.

I have said that emotions are construals, but in reflection on my examples you may think I would have better called them beliefs or judgments. After all, were not all the different emotions that Hank might have experienced out of concern for his plants *beliefs* about what was happening or likely to happen to the plants? He believed a storm was threatening their safety, or that the danger had passed, or that a neighbor had rescued them, or that the teen-ager was responsibly damaging them. Of course one *could* say that he construed them as threatened, rescued, etc.; but wouldn't "believed" be a more precise term?

I think not. But before I show this, let us reflect a bit on what a construal, in my sense of the word, is. The following figure is found on p. 295 of Joseph Jastrow's *Fact and Fable in Psychology*:

It can be seen as a picture of a duck's head or as a picture of a rabbit's. When you first glanced at it you may have seen it only as a duck's head. Then I told you that it can be seen as a rabbit's, and perhaps you looked at it again, searched the figure a bit, maybe turned it on its side; and then the rabbit's head *appeared* to you. That is, the experience of the duck-rabbit as a rabbit's head *came* to you, came over you; the rabbit's head *emerged* in the figure, much as your "view" of somebody as offensive, or pitiful, or generous, or conniving, sometimes comes over you all of a sudden. After you have managed to see the figure both ways, with a little practice, you can see it as one or the other *at will*. There is a sense of "see" in which, seeing it in these different ways, you do *not* see anything different; and what you see in this sense is not subject to your will. That is, if your eyes are open and functioning normally and if the figure is well lit, you will see the figure of the duck-rabbit, and you have no choice about it. But after you have learned the trick, you *do* have a choice about how to *construe* it, and upon your choice depends whether you have one or the other of the two very different experiences of the figure.

Now I want to suggest that one aspect of having an emotion is very much like "seeing" the duck in the duck-rabbit. (Obviously, this experience is not an emotion, and the aspect that is missing is the concern: the sight of the duck in the duck-rabbit doesn't impinge, typically, on any concern of the con-struer.) To be indignant is to see myself or someone close to me as intentionally injured by someone, in a matter of some concern to myself. To be in despair is to see my life, which I deeply desire to be meaningful, as holding nothing, or nothing of importance, for me. To be envious is to see myself as losing against some competitor in a competition upon which I am staking my self-esteem. To feel guilty is to see myself as having offended against a moral or quasi-moral standard to which I subscribe.

In the case of the Christian emotions, the terms of the seeing are provided by the Christian story. To experience peace with God is to see God as a reconciled enemy. To experience hope is to see one's own future in the eternity and righteousness of God's kingdom. To be Christianly grateful is to see various precious gifts, such as existence, sustenance, and redemption, as be-stowed by God. Because emotions are construals, and construals always require some "terms," and the "terms" of the Christian emotions are provided by the Christian story, there is a necessary connection between the Christian emotions and the Christian story. So people who don't want to think of the spiritual life in terms of emotions and feelings because they believe that emo-tions are "subjective" and cut off from "doctrine" and thinking can lay their fears to rest. Emotions are no less tied to concepts than arguments and beliefs are.

IT is important to Christians that emotions are partially within people's control, that they can be *commanded*. Jesus says that everyone who is angry with his brother shall be liable to judg-ment. Paul tells the Romans to rejoice with those who rejoice and weep with those who weep, and he tells the Philippians to rejoice in the Lord always. When he says that love is not jealous, or irritable, or resentful, he seems to assume that these feelings are broadly within the control of his readers. Being resentful is not like being five foot six or having congenitally bad teeth.

The fact that emotions are construals goes a long way to-ward explaining how we have control over them, and also why we sometimes fail to control them when we try. (I am talking about a genuine control of *emotion*, and not just the suppression of the *behavior* which threatens to issue from an emotion.) To succeed in bringing myself into a certain emotional state is to succeed in coming to see my situation in certain terms. To succeed in dispelling an emotion, I must somehow get myself to cease to see the situation in one set of terms, and probably must get myself to see it in different terms. But "seeing" is a little bit like imagining. Sometimes my mother's face appears to my imagination uninvited, sometimes I can imagine it if asked to do so, and sometimes I can't succeed in imagining it, no matter how hard I try. It is the same with figures like the duck-rabbit, if they are a little more complicated than the duck-rabbit. And it is the same with emotions. Sometimes I am hopeful without trying, sometimes I can make myself hopeful by trying to see promise in my situation, and sometimes I cannot make myself hopeful no matter how hard I try.

In *The Principles of Psychology* William James makes the following commonsense observation about how emotions can be controlled through behavior:

> Everyone knows how panic is increased by flight, and how the giving way to the symptoms of grief or anger increases those passions themselves. . . . In rage, it is notorious how we "work ourselves up" to a climax by repeated outbreaks of expression. . . . Whistling to keep up courage is no mere figure of speech. On the other hand, sit all day in a moping posture, sigh, and reply to everything with a dismal voice, and your melancholy lingers. (vol. II, pp. 462–63)

In other words, if you want to encourage an emotion, *act* in conformity with it, even if you don't initially feel like it; and if you want to discourage one, refuse to act in conformity with it, or better yet, act in conformity with a contrary emotion. This of course does not always work, but I am impressed how often it does work, and am sure it would work even more often if we practiced the policy more assiduously and self-consciously.

My suggestion that en.otions are construals will help us to understand why this way of controlling our emotions sometimes works (and also why it sometimes does not). The key is this: when I *act* angry, it is much easier and more natural to construe the situation as one to which anger is the appropriate response. Let us say that I have explained a point to a student a number of times, and he has now come to my office complaining that he still does not understand. By this time I am inclined to see him as obnoxious, and as imposing unnecessarily on my time and energy. But I sit down with him beside me at my desk, and explain the point once more by making a diagram on a piece of scratch paper. He still does not (or will not) understand, and there is something in his voice which seems to accuse me of making things too complicated. I am inclined to rebuke him sharply and send him out of my office summarily. But instead, applying James's advice, I lay my hand on his shoulder in a fatherly way and speak some gentle words of encouragement to him. And the anger which was threatening to come over me is dispelled.

The reason this strategy is often effective is that becoming angry with someone necessarily involves construing him as obnoxious, offensive, or some such thing. And it is much more *difficult* to see someone as obnoxious if I have my hand resting affectionately on his shoulder and I am speaking gentle words of encouragement to him than if I am yelling at him and throwing him out of my office. The reason it is not always effective is that it is not *impossible* to construe someone as obnoxious while assuming the opposite posture toward him. Sometimes that initial construal just seems so right, and so heavily superior to every alternative construal, that no amount of dissonant behavior will change the original construal. But our emotions are intractable less often than we would like to imagine.

C. S. Lewis, I think, somewhere advises this: If you want to become a Christian, but find it presently impossible to believe the things Christians believe, you may begin by *acting* like a Christian. No need to start out with anything as heavy as belief. Just sing praises to God along with the Christians, imitate them in their posture toward suffering, join with them in their life of compassion and sacrifice. You will begin to construe the world as a Christian does, to experience Christianity from within. And who knows? That way of looking at things may eventually come to seem so heavily superior to every other way, that you find, one day, that you believe. When that happens, your disposition to the Christian emotions will have become firm.

Earlier in this chapter I asked whether we shouldn't say that emotions are beliefs, rather than construals. By now, I hope my reason for saying no to this question is obvious. Beliefs are dispositions, whereas emotions are occurrences in consciousness.

A Christian's belief that eternal life awaits him is not something that *occurs* at various times of the day. He does not cease to believe it when he concentrates his mind on a mathematical puzzle or when he falls asleep. He may believe this and yet, if he is not very faithfully practicing his Christianity, go for days or weeks without thinking about it. But if he isn't at all attending to eternity, then he cannot be experiencing Christian hope as an emotion. For hope is a way of *looking* at things. He may, of course, be a person who is disposed to be hopeful; that is, he may be the sort of person who *would* experience hope if something stimulated him to do so. But hope itself, like the other emotions, involves setting one's mind on the things of the Spirit. This is why belief is not enough for spirituality. Christians must not only believe, but also must learn to *attend* to the things of God. For only in doing so will they begin to bear the fruits of God's Spirit.

❋ 3 ❋
Something Eternal in the Self

IN the last chapter we inquired briefly about human emotion, both what it is and how much control we have over it. We are interested in these questions because we believe that several of the Christian virtues are emotions, and we wish to understand these better and learn what we may do to cultivate them. I argued that emotions are ways of "seeing" things that concern us in one way or another. The Christian emotions, accordingly are concerned ways of viewing things through the "lenses" of Christian teaching—that is, the doctrines and stories of the Christian tradition. But the "view" that a person takes of things is a fruit of the Holy Spirit—that is, a heartfelt emotion—only if it is grounded in the concerns which are fundamental to Christianity. University religion teachers, especially if they are "theologians," may become adept at construing the world in Christian terms. That is, they imaginatively get "inside" Christianity (or indeed any religion) so as to "understand" it and to help their students "understand" it. But it would be absurd to take this kind of mental virtuosity for Christian faith, or the experiences that arise from it as the fruits of the Spirit. Their *academic* familiarity with Christianity is not to be confused with the *personal* concern of the Christian and the seriousness which her Christian construals have (even though the academic and the personal may be combined in the same person). It is *concerns* which allow the Christian language and thinking to get a grip on us. They give the Christian teachings *traction*.

In the next three chapters I want to explore the passion that is the basis of the Christian emotions. The account I give is in a sense evolutionary. I begin at the bottom of the scale, with the suggestion of a yearning for eternity or for something abstractly resembling the kingdom of God upon which the Christian pins his hopes; what I describe in this chapter is not the Christian passion, but something out of which the Christian passion is capable of developing. In the following two chapters, I work gradually toward the description of a passion which is fully adequate and fitted to the Christian teachings. Something like this evolution might occur in the life of individuals, but I am not claiming that all Christians actually go through something like this development or the thought processes that underlie it. Many different patterns of development can lead to a mature Christian passion. My account is therefore not designed to reflect individual development; it is, instead, a framework by which to organize the psychological and conceptual points I wish to make about the nature and growth of the passion which underlies the Christian spiritual life.

KIERKEGAARD'S Anti-Climacus comments that "as a rule, imagination is the medium for the process of infinitizing" (*Sickness Unto Death*, p. 30). By "infinitizing" he refers to a process in the maturation of the individual's self-consciousness. It is a process by which the person becomes aware of a dimension of himself, of his capacity to will and of his needs, which sets him apart from animals and perhaps children and other living things that live entirely in terms of their "earthly" relationships. An essential and very important dimension of the human self—in terms of his needs and his obligations—is established by the fact that he can soar in thought beyond the immediate circumstances of his life. This may seem a small thing, before one meditates on it; but it has enormous consequences for what a human self is.

Human life, even when it is far from intellectual, is fundamentally a life of the mind. The posture of the mind, as the Stoics knew very well, determines so much about the character of the individual's life. Of course not all exercises of the imagination are "infinitizing," but there is in every exercise of imagination the potential for, and a certain amount of pressure toward, an "infinitizing" movement.

Humans are, as far as we know, the only animals that can be transported by a novel or a movie into another world, with its loves and hates, enchantments and terrors, cozy comforts and unnerving suspense. They alone can know, ten years in advance, that the moon will be full on a given day, or sixty years in advance, that they will one day molder in the ground. Only a human life can be shaped by an ideal, such as the life of Christ, or an ideology, such as Marxism, or an obsession, like making money. Only for a human being can a multi-colored piece of fabric flapping in the wind "mean" the complex of geography and culture which is America. By imagination the actor brings himself to see the world through Hamlet's eyes. By imagination the richest woman in the world may put herself in the shoes of a beggar dying in the streets of Calcutta, and so be moved by compassion. A man dying in a prison cell can be happy, because he sees himself as suffering for a righteous cause, while another in the bloom of health, free and surrounded by opportunities, may blow his brains out because he feels his mother doesn't love him.

L ET me describe some exercises of the imagination which Christians will take as manifesting the Godward side of our nature. Then I want to consider some questions about them.

I went to the funeral of an old lady who had been a friend of my wife and me. Then I came home and hugged Elizabeth, my wife, whose womb was becoming very full with our first child (later to be known as Nathan). I said, "In seventy-seven years (that was the age of the lady) this unborn child will be weak and wrinkled and bent over too." The image of that rosy-cheeked, perfectly coiffured, pickled corpse lying so still among the satin and the lilies served to focus an undeniable aspect of that little kicker whose plumpness and gurgling and play would soon delight his daddy. It served to contain in a single moment of thought the life span of that little person who was already becoming dear to me. To survey a life that is very important to me, to catch it all in a moment, is to get a sense of the futility of it—if that is all there is to it. It is to feel a kind of desperate emptiness about it, a cosmic sadness, and perhaps to reach out in longing for another world in which the beauty of life should be given its due. My own experience has been that the entire business of bringing a child into the world and rearing him, of contemplating his naive enthusiasms and the beauty of his little body, is an occasion for many desperate sensations of the futility of life apart from God.

The prophet Isaiah says,

A voice says, "Cry!"
   And I said, "What shall I cry?"
All flesh is grass,
   and all its beauty is like the flower of the field.
The grass withers, the flower fades,
   when the breath of the Lord blows upon it;
   and surely the people is grass.
The grass withers, the flower fades;
   but the word of our God will stand for ever.

Isaiah distils in a simple image a truth which can never be far
from the mind of a thinking adult. You are grass: your life is a
blooming and a fading, a flourishing and a withering, a birthing
and a dying. This thought frequents the human mind—though
mostly in its recesses. Walking to work, peeling potatoes, chat-
ting at a cozy party over a glass of wine, holding hands with
your spouse, playing silly games with your children. And there's
the lurking thought: flesh fading and disappearing, withering
grass.

But there are times, too, when this truth comes home with
special vigor, and what is only a nagging uneasiness changes
into outright terror: the sudden "absurd" death of a friend, a
close brush with accidental death in the midst of play, a pain
which I interpret as the first symptom of a dread disease. Sometimes a more purely reflective event can trigger this look at reality. My mind, otherwise accustomed to cunning self-deception
in matters relating to death, is sometimes thrust into honesty by
reading or hearing about astronomy. This probably works only
because I do not very often think astronomically; if I did I suppose I would soon become jaded and "objective" in my thinking
here too, the way doctors and army lieutenants and funeral directors do. But for me, occasionally thinking about the vast ex-
panses of time that it takes for the stars to do their things, or
even for the planets to go through certain of their cycles, gives
me a visceral new perspective on the time from my birth to my
death. For example, Pluto takes about three or four human life-
times to revolve once around the sun. And it goes round and
round and round. My entire life is to Pluto what the fraction of
a year is to my life—approximately three months.

It is easy to survey the life of a blade of grass: *of course* it
springs up fresh and firm and green in the springtime and then

withers with the winter freeze, and rots in the following season. That's just how it goes with grass (as can be seen by a being who survives the changes of many seasons—maybe seventy or eighty or even ninety such changes). But astronomy stimulates the imagination to take a larger perspective, something like Isaiah's. From here I comprehend, as in a tiny droplet of the universe's time, that moment in the process of flourishing and disappearance which belongs to my very own flesh. All flesh (*my* flesh) is grass. But here I'm not inclined to say, "*Of course* that's how my life is. That's just the way it is with flesh." No, when I apply it to myself, the thought of withering appals.

A person who is inclined to view his own life honestly and admit without casting his eyes aside that all flesh is grass will welcome the thought that there is an enduring rock amidst the flux of things. Isaiah's preaching, if we really hear it, touches our deepest need. He ministers to the worry that pervades all our thoughts. But why does he say that the *word* of our God endures forever? Wouldn't it be enough to proclaim that *God* is eternal, that he stands forever?

Probably not, if Isaiah intends to speak comfort and good tidings to those who are dying. To a very philosophical mind, maybe it would be some comfort to believe that, amidst the flux of things, at least God endures forever. But I doubt it. Wouldn't such a philosophical attitude really be a cover-up for despair? Most of us, anyway, wouldn't find much in the doctrine of God's eternity to feed on, especially if it seemed that God wasn't well disposed toward us and that he didn't include us in his enduring. But in the Christian perspective Isaiah is preaching the really good news that God's loving disposition toward us—his word of mercy and comfort—endures forever and cannot be turned aside.

ANOTHER way this kind of truth gets focused is by reflecting on the activities that fill our lives with meaning. We all know what a miserable thing ennui is. Having suffered through long, tedious school assignments in which we could see no purpose, or a nearly eternal night twiddling our thumbs in the Detroit bus depot, we see that meaningful activity is a kind of food for our souls. The emptiness and impatience we feel at such times show that we need to be able to engross ourselves in activities, to *give* ourselves to them more or less wholeheartedly, if they are to fill our lives with meaning. In moments when our activity seems pointless to us, or when we're inactive because we can see no purpose in doing anything, consciousness becomes a burden. No activity will fill us unless we have an interest in it, and an interest cannot fill us if we do not see ourselves as making some headway toward accomplishing its goal.

Most of us succeed in finding foci for those interests which fill our moments with meaning. We find this in our jobs, our families, our hobbies, in music or competitive sports, in artistic creation or politics, in church work, cooking, sewing, woodworking, firewood gathering, and scholarship. When one such activity begins to bore us, we try to find ourselves in still others, sometimes wandering far and experimenting much in the process. If the activity which becomes empty has been a major focus of our life (e.g., a profession or a family which has now grown up), so that it seems hopeless to find a replacement for it, the emptiness can become a generalized despair. The whole of life begins to feel sort of like that night in the Detroit bus depot, only without the comfort of the prospect that daylight will come when the Toronto bus will carry one into a context of meaningful activities once more.

Even the most trivial activity, if my consciousness of purpose is sufficiently monopolized by it, can provide momentary significance. If I am absorbed in splitting a stubborn piece of oak for the fireplace, then for that moment, and insofar as larger thoughts don't enter in, my life is filled with meaning. The hitch here is that it's virtually impossible for somebody to be *entirely* absorbed in activities of the moment. Because she is a reflective being, she is always at least peripherally conscious of a larger view of this moment, and always prone to ask, "Why am I doing this?" "Is this activity to any purpose?" That is, she is always, with one degree of consciousness or another, backing off from the present moment and surveying and evaluating her activities. Often she is not very conscious of going further with this evaluation than the answer "I'm chopping this wood because I want a fire this evening." If the question, however, is not about firewood but about a career, the evaluation will come closer to being a survey of her life as a whole: "Are the activities which most permanently and pervasively lend meaning to my life really *worthy*? That is, worthy of me, and worthy in themselves? Am I happy with the kind of happiness I derive from them? Is it enough?" And very often such reflection has time and death in view. Perhaps she looks over her past decade with its achievements and pleasures, and says to herself, "Possibly I have two, or three, or four such decades left to me. Is *that* what my life amounts to?"

And if the answer comes back, "Yes, that is what it amounts to, and that is *all*, there is nothing more, that's the *whole* story," then the sensation is one of despair. It is in such moments of surveying insight that we sense the emptiness of a life which is not rooted in a time-frame larger than our seventy or eighty years nor aimed at a *telos* higher than accomplishments, comforts, money, pleasure, and applause. Thus some very meaningful activities (when considered in their momentary or at least narrower context) are suspended in a web of meaninglessness, unless the individual believes that what she does she does to some eternal glory and in the service (however humbly and indirectly) of some eternal order of things. Because of our ability and compulsion to *survey* our lives, "to see them for what they're worth," meaninglessness is the destiny of human consciousness — except in the context of eternity.

You may want to address to me the words a certain Mr. Edwards addressed to Dr. Johnson: " 'You are a philosopher, Dr. Johnson. I have tried too in my time to be a philosopher; but, I don't know how, cheerfulness was always breaking in.' True, many people have the experiences you describe, but your tendency to dwell on them just shows what a morbid person you are. Why emphasize negative things like meaninglessness and death and cosmic fretfulness? Let us stress the joys that can be had, the simple pleasures of work and play, hearty conversation, good food, and lovemaking! If we cultivated the kind of thoughts you have described we'd poison what good things there are in life. Your morbidity comes from an unwillingness to accept life as it is — indeed from a lack of creaturely humility. Besides, a great deal of our life is free from these troublesome experiences. Most of the time we are happily engaged in our work and play, nicely focused down on the present moment where we find meaning and are distracted from the thought of death. We should cultivate this immersion in the present moment, because it is there that we find our happiness, and there that we most naturally live our life. By contrast, the experiences you have described are farfetched and unnatural and, in the healthy individual, infrequent."

Thank you for your impassioned objections. Let me sort them a bit, so as to answer them one by one. First, you say that anyone who dwells on these experiences is *morbid*. But this is surely not true. Some persons who show no other signs of mental illness are well acquainted with these thoughts. And these experiences lack one of the crucial marks of psychological disease, namely that of distorting reality. They are not at all like the case of the sixty-five-pound victim of anorexia nervosa who believes that if she eats more heartily she will get fat, or that of the paranoiac who believes that everyone he meets is plotting his downfall. The person who reckons by vivid imagination with the fact of his own death and considers what consequences this has for the meaningfulness of a life devoted to getting money and fame may have a balanced view of his condition. It is *he* who is realistic and honest, not the person who systematically denies these disturbing thoughts. It might well be argued that sickness lies in the *in*ability to acknowledge the fact of one's own death, and to feel the meaninglessness of a life that is totally immersed in the passing show. If, however, we hesitate to call most of humanity sick, we can at least say that they are not very clear, emotionally, about the nature of their life.

But perhaps when you called me morbid, you didn't mean literally that I am suffering from mental disease, but only that I have a rather gloomy outlook. And maybe you are even willing to pay the price of lying to yourself to secure a happier disposition. But of course I am not counseling that you poison your life with gloomy thoughts. The Christian is not stuck with despair and meaninglessness when she sees that she is left unfulfilled if life in this present time and space is the whole story. For her it's *not* the whole story. It is for this reason that she can hear in the experiences I have described the voice of God calling her away from a life of immersion in the present passing world, calling her to attach herself in faith and hope and love to himself and his eternal kingdom.

No doubt most Christians have a long way to go in getting

ourselves attached to God and his kingdom and detached from the world, and so the thought of dying and the survey of our life's meaning *does* seem gloomy to us, and maybe even terrifying. No one who understands will deny that becoming a Christian is a painful process; but neither will he deny that it's worth the price of discipline. And so the Christian who opts to turn away from such experiences as I have described in favor of a "happier disposition" in which he continues in the semiillusion that he will never die has not only chosen dishonesty. He has also chosen a happiness which will let him down, a superficial, passing happiness, fit for animals perhaps, but deadly when adopted by a creature who is spirit.

He who immerses himself in the passing show has chosen a kind of happiness which lets him down. And it doesn't just let him down on his deathbed, so to speak, but creates a life of anxiety and despair all along the way. If he is pretty good at self-deception, he may seem happy to himself and to others. But if he ever looks back clearly on his mental state during those years and sees through to the bottom of his immersion in the passing show, he will have to admit that he was in a more or less dulled state of misery, restlessness, and fear. Escape along this route fails because, after all, it is not possible to immerse oneself totally in present moments. Horses and dogs and porcupines, lacking the mental apparatus for having values and ideals, and for scanning themselves from birth to death and beyond, necessarily take the moments of their lives as they come. Their "place" is the present moment, and so they have nothing like the liabilities to error and unhappiness, and the spiritual needs, that we human beings have. Walt Whitman once expressed a wistful longing for this simplicity of animal consciousness:

> I think I could turn and live with animals, they are so
>   placid and self-contain'd,
> I stand and look at them long and long.
> They do not sweat and whine about their condition,
> They do not lie awake in the dark and weep for their
>   sins,
> They do not make me sick discussing their duty to God,
> Not one is dissatisfied, not one is demented with the
>   mania of owning things,

Not one kneels to another, nor to his kind that lived
    thousands of years ago,
Not one is respectable or unhappy over the whole earth.
               ("Song of Myself," section 32)

The key is in that word "self-contain'd": the animals are not
subject to our deepest miseries because they are naturally "immediate." They do not live beyond themselves, by virtue of reflection and imagination, as human beings do. We, by contrast,
lack the option of *not* so scanning our lives and looking for
meaning, try as we may to avoid doing so.

We do of course have some control over our imagination.
We can concentrate on selected thoughts, and disallow or dis-
tract ourselves from others. If we did not have this power,
St. Paul's admonition to set our minds on the things of the Spirit
and Christ's warning not to lust sexually would be absurd because unobeyable. But at the same time we are passively subject
to our imagination. Thoughts "haunt" us; they spring up uninvited; they are triggered sometimes by the most unlikely events.
And that surveying function of the imagination, in which we
confront our death and the meaninglessness of a life bound-
within-finitude, dogs us. It is perpetually present, if not quite
in consciousness, then just below the surface.

Being a coward, I may shrink from such thoughts and try
to drive them away. "Just don't think that way," I tell myself,
"and everything will be all right." And I may succeed in this,
over the short haul. I can open the Sears Roebuck catalog and
drift into a reverie about some new tools for my workshop. Or
call up a friend and see if we can get a racquetball court. I can,
self-deceitfully, compare my professional success with that of a
less aggressive colleague—as though *that* were some solution to
the problem of cosmic meaninglessness! Or go out for a jog or
eat health foods or remind myself that I live in a small town
where the air and water are clean, or dwell on the fact that there
isn't much heart disease and cancer in my family history—as
though ten or twenty years more of life were some solution to
the problem of death! Or I may rest my hope on my son's car-
rying on my ideals and my projects—as if, even if that unlikely
event occurred, the same problem doesn't arise in his case and
that of his son and so on. The difficulty with such expedients of
thought is that they are all so patently beside the point.

And even if I am morally degenerate enough to be comfortable with the lie involved in them, still they will not save me long from despair, for my imagination will exercise me in the presence of death, even if I refuse to exercise my imagination in the presence of it. God has got my scent again and is trailing close behind. I lay me down to sleep, and in the still darkness somewhere just below the surface of consciousness swims that surveying imagination. The ominous truth from which I seek to guard my vision glimmers faintly in the waters of darkness. Then, drowsy, I let my guard down and it comes splashing up to meet me: the spectre of my death and the meaninglessness of my life is solid and clear and terrifying. I rouse myself, shake my head and try to come back to the "real" world by turning on the light. I sit there, propped in a more mastering position with my pillow against the headboard, and think again about how successful my career really is, and how healthy I am, after all, for a man of forty, and what a bright little son I have. It is something of a comfort to be back to reality. But now I am afraid to put my head on the pillow again, afraid that spectre will swim back toward me. So I get up and work for an hour on my income tax return, and gradually the impression of terror gets fainter. And finally, before I go back to bed, I take a sleeping pill, to make sure that this time I sink *totally* into unconsciousness.

SOMETHING you pointed out in your earlier criticism of my position was that by immersing ourselves in our finite life, and distracting our attention from the issues that would draw us into the arms of the eternal, we would express a kind of creaturely humility and at the same time keep from poisoning the bit of happiness that we *can* find in life. I have suggested that your approach has a couple of liabilities: it is dishonest, and besides that, bound to fail. But now I want to claim that a forthright acknowledgment of the eternal element in us, indeed a *cultivation* of the sense of our death and the meaninglessness-in-themselves of the activities of this life, does not have the liabilities that you say it has.

Let us start with the matter of creaturely humility. If we are creatures with a religious tendency (as it seems pretty obvious that we are), then humility would be a matter of accepting our-

selves as *that*. It would be an exaggerated humility, wouldn't it,
if we whose hearts are restless till they rest in the eternal denied
that fact about ourselves and sought to become more like the
dogs and horses and porcupines of this world. Creaturely humility is all relative to whatever kind of creature is under consideration. If dogs can accept themselves quite happily without
any relationship to something beyond this present world, then
humility, for them, is quite nicely expressed by a total immersion
in this world. But there *is* something eternal in the human self,
a deep-rooted longing that is difficult, if not impossible, to eradicate. And if one takes it seriously, as Christians must, then to
try to eradicate it must appear as the most perilous and foolish
thing a person can do. Cultivating this restlessness, and letting
ourselves become transparent in it, is not a proud seeking to be
something that we are not, but is just the natural expression of
the kind of creatures that we are. In seeking the eternal, or
welcoming it passionately when it comes to us, we are not being
like the emperor who wants, absurdly, to be a god, or the ex-
istentialist, who wants, equally absurdly, to be his own moral
law giver. We are being much more like the collie who is just
gloriously glad to be a dog.

Your other objection is that, by dwelling on the kind of
thoughts that I am discussing in this chapter, we will poison
what little happiness can be found in human life. I answer that
it is only by finding and assimilating a life view in which these
thoughts can be honestly accommodated that we can *prevent*
our natural pleasures from being poisoned. For the truth is that
the most exquisite moments in the life of a worldling (and of a
worldly Christian) are often deeply compromised. A moment of
success in our work, the exhilaration of health in a session of
vigorous physical exercise, a moment of intense tenderness with
our spouse, a romp with the children, a Christmas feast with
family and friends—the very intensity of these pleasures tends
to beckon those lurking thoughts to the surface of consciousness. But the anxiety we feel in the face of death is the consequence of our investing *this* life (from which we must die) with
ultimate significance. The despair we feel when forced to reckon
with the vanity of all our activities and pleasures is the result of
our according *ultimate* significance to those activities and pleasures—to their being for us the *whole* story, or the *center* of the

story. If we could manage to see this life as a stage in an eternal life, then it could be accepted honestly and gladly for what it is. If we could see the significance of our present activities and pleasures as deriving from a context beyond this present one of flowering and fading, they could be honestly enjoyed for what they are, no less and no more. If on the other hand we have no larger expectation in terms of which to interpret this life, then since we are creatures who cannot escape our surveying imagination and our deeper longings, embitterment dwells on our doorstep. And we live in constant fear of stepping out into the open.

Christianity is, among other things, the wonderfully good news that this life is not our whole story. We have been redeemed for an eternal kingdom by a Lord who is the first fruits of the resurrection from the dead. The few years that we live in this body (that blink in the history of Pluto, as it were) are a kind of pilgrimage, a sojourn, a preparatory trip on the way to something much greater. They should be understood as school years. When we are in school we are quite clear (if we are serious students) that our central activities there are directed to something beyond school. The quality of our life there is going to be tested by that life for which our school life is a preparation; and the quality of our school life will determine, to some extent, the quality of life after school. We say that school life is a preparation for *real* life; and so the serious student is conscious of a certain unreality of the present. For the Christian, similarly, this present existence is provisional. He is aware that every activity he undertakes is schooling for something else—that it is all *directed* toward a higher end. The way he comports himself at work and play, the way he relates to other people, the use he makes of the goods at his disposal: these are all exercises in preparation for real life. (Of course, to continue the analogy and balance the account, it needs to be said that school life *is* in many ways real life; it if weren't, it wouldn't be a good preparation for the future.)

Such a consciousness is pure health and pure honesty for a being with a surveying imagination such as man has. In such a consciousness time and eternity are related as they ought to be: time is given its full significance (which is great) but not more than that. It is understood entirely in its relationship to eternity.

Time is the place where our salvation is to be worked out, and so it is taken with the seriousness of fear and trembling (a far greater seriousness, in one sense, than any worldling can take toward it). But since its seriousness is that of a preparation for something else, it can in another sense be passed off somewhat lightly, with a sense of humor and a readiness to depart.

For a person whose roots have been thoroughly transplanted from the present soil into that of eternity, who dances lightly on the surface of the earth and so is ready to leave at a moment's notice, there would be little point in dwelling on the thought of death. Sad to say, however, this mind-set is rarely to be found among those who profess Christianity. Most churchgoers are as deeply rooted in this world, and thus as deeply in despair, as those who profess no such hope. For this reason dwelling on experiences like the ones I described earlier is a necessary and healthy exercise for us. We must become friends of despair if we are to be drawn above it to genuine and heartfelt hope. Far from being an exercise in morbidity, a deepening acquaintance with our death and with the vanity of human wishes is for our worldly hearts a needed path to perfect health.

❋ 4 ❋
The Death of Ivan Ilych

THERE is another source of discomfort with what I have out-lined in the last chapter. People with a certain deeply moral view of the world, which has been with us in different forms since the eighteenth century, may feel that the fear of eternal discon-tinuation is hardly worthy of us and is, or ought to be, com-pletely submerged in another concern. And ultimately, for this heroic stance, the prospect of absolute annihilation is the gra-cious beneficence of the universe towards us. Wittgenstein has this to say towards the end of his *Tractatus*:

> Not only is there no guarantee of the temporal immor-tality of the human soul, that is to say of its eternal survival after death; but, in any case, this assumption completely fails to accomplish the purpose for which it has always been intended. Or is some riddle solved by my surviving forever? Is not this eternal life itself as much of a riddle as our present life? The solution of the riddle of life in space and time lies *outside* space and time.

It sounds a little odd to say that the doctrine of immortality was intended to solve a "riddle." But the thinking seems to be this: it seems to us that life *ought* to be immortal. Indeed, until we reach a certain age and experience, we probably live on the practical assumption that we *are* immortal. But then it becomes clear that we are not. For the individua₁ the passion for life is so great that it seems to him a contradiction that he is going to die. Then the doctrine of immortality comes along and resolves this contradiction by asserting that what seems to be the death of the person is really only the sloughing off of the body.

But, responds Wittgenstein, this is not really a solution, not primarily because there seems to be no reason to believe it, but because it trades on a shallow analysis of the problem. Our life is compromised not by death, but by something lying in *us*, within the power of our will. To a superficial view it may look as though all our troubles would be over if only we could live a healthy life without end. But what we want, down deeper, is not just *more* life, but a *worthwhile* life. Or, more precisely, a *worthy* life. The life we are presently living is unworthy, and no extension of it beyond the grave will solve the problem that that fact poses. What stings about life is not fundamentally that it comes to a temporal end, but that we are guilty, that we have failed to become what we ought, have failed to achieve worthiness. The riddle of life is constituted not by our mortality, but by our unrighteousness.

We cannot but admire the seriousness of this attitude. It is so thoroughly ethical that it can look in the teeth of the most terrifying natural facts and say, as it were, "their terror is nothing in comparison with what I feel when I compare what I am with what I ought to be." How much more penetrating is this attitude than the cringing, whining view that we are essentially victims of fate, whether fate takes the form of nature, the Soviet Union, big business, the hippies, our department head, the military establishment, the drug runners, or the incompetents in the White House—and that we, by contrast, while we may have made a few mistakes, are essentially innocent! Wittgenstein asks what is the apple that's causing all the rotting in the barrel, and answers by pointing his thumb at his own heart. And he invites each of us to do the same. In this understanding of things, the sins of others cease to be inscrutable abysses of alien darkness and look instead like mirrors in which we see our deepest selves. This outlook produces not the self-righteousness which accuses and alienates the other and confirms us in our evil, but instead a sense of solidarity with all persons. Hitler is somebody *I* could have been, given the appropriate temptations.

But this is not an easy, gliding solidarity such as you find among those who need each other for mutual survival or profit— the members of a ball team, or a corporation, or a nation at war. It is rather a solidarity in which each, looking at the other, sees in himself the most stinging riddle of life. And paradoxically, in this pain of self-accusation and self-alienation a person finds, unstably, something of the righteousness of which he has bereaved himself. For in it he has been humbled and reconciled, in a way, to every brother and sister he meets, in whatever condition they may be. Envy, vanity, pride, enmity, and selfishness have been tortured from his heart, and something not wholly unlike love has been put in their place. But I say "unstably" because this resolution of the riddle by the sting of the riddle itself is at best fleeting and partial, and the individual who has been momentarily "saved" by his contrition soon falls back again into the attitudes that make him such a riddle to himself. He must look elsewhere than to the strength of his moral passion for a savior from himself.

Some thinkers have thought to find in the prospect of absoluted death this savior. Thus the interpretation of death which I attempt to explicate in the last chapter is, according to them, erroneous and morally degrading. The prospect of death should not be taken as an occasion for cutting oneself loose from earth and pinning one's hopes on eternal life in God's kingdom. This is only to short-circuit the process of salvation, to give an illusion of cure rather than to effect a real one. Only by facing absolute death can we gain the character which the morally sensitive person sees to be the single thing in life worth achieving. So in the present chapter I want to consider this objection to the direction our thought took in Chapter 3.

LEO Tolstoy's short story "The Death of Ivan Ilych" details the kind of spirituality I want to discuss. All my quotations are taken from *The Death of Ivan Ilych and Other Stories*.

Ivan Ilych is an ordinary man of the middle class, a civil servant who has been rather successful in working his way up through the ranks. His life is entirely devoted to pleasure: "The pleasures connected with his work were pleasures of ambition; his social pleasures were those of vanity; but Ivan Ilych's greatest pleasure was playing bridge" (p. 119). From his superiors Ivan Ilych, who is fastidious about proprieties, derives the standards by which he lives. From those who are placed under him he derives his sense of power: "and he liked to treat them politely, almost as comrades, as if he were letting them feel that he who had the power to crush them was treating them in this simple, friendly way" (p. 107).

He marries a pretty young woman, and for a while married life enhances his pleasures. But then a child comes, and his wife, bored from being cooped up all the time at home, becomes demanding, jealous, and irascible, poisoning Ivan Ilych's life for a time. He meets this problem with a well considered strategy:

> He only required [of married life] those conveniences — dinner at home, housewife, and bed — which it could give him, and above all that propriety of external forms required by public opinion. For the rest he looked for light-hearted pleasure and propriety, and was very thankful when he found them, but if he met with antagonism and querulousness he at once retired into his separate fenced-off world of official duties, where he found satisfaction. (pp. 110–111)

Thus Ivan Ilych and his wife come to be more and more like two ships passing in the night, but he succeeds nicely in keeping his life pleasant.

After a minor setback in his career, he is promoted to a well-paying position in Petersburg. He buys a comfortable house, and so intense is his interest in the decoration of it that he even sometimes finds his mind wandering while he presides in the court. One day, standing on a ladder demonstrating to the upholsterer how he wants the hangings draped, he slips and falls, knocking his side against the knob of the window frame.

At first it seems he has sustained only a bruise, but over the next few weeks the pain in his side becomes increasingly bothersome, and he begins to experience a strange taste in his mouth. He becomes irritable and quarrelsome, and visits doctor after doctor, who prescribe various medicines and give conflicting opinions. Ivan Ilych becomes less and less able to convince himself that he is not dying. The activities in which he formerly delighted seem to have lost their point. One evening at cards "his partner said 'No trumps' and supported him with two diamonds. What more could be wished for? It ought to be jolly and lively. They would make a grand slam. But suddenly Ivan Ilych was conscious of that gnawing pain, that taste in his mouth, and it seemed ridiculous that in such circumstances he should be pleased to make a grand slam" (p. 126).

His impending death brings on a sense of loneliness which is the most tormenting part of the ordeal. At work, he perceives that the chief significance of his imminent demise is that certain of his colleagues will gain promotions. His family and friends continue their round of social engagements, their outings to the theatre, their dinner parties at home. His daughter becomes engaged to marry. They evade the subject of his death, and to a great extent evade him too. His wife pretends that if he would only follow the doctor's orders, he would be just fine. He begins to see that because he is dying, he is an annoyance to his family. He is taking the edge off their fun: " 'Is it our fault?' Lisa said to her mother. 'It's as if we were to blame! I am sorry for papa, but why should we be tortured?' " (p. 151). What to Ivan Ilych is the most awful and cataclysmic event in the history of the universe is to these self-centered pleasure seekers a minor vexation to be addressed with the deceits of convention: "The awful, terrible act of his dying was, he could see, reduced by those about him to the level of a casual, unpleasant and almost indecorous incident (as if someone entered a drawing-room diffusing an unpleasant odour) and this was done by that very decorum which he had served all his life long" (pp. 137–138).

There are two exceptions in Ivan Ilych's house. His young son seems genuinely to have pity on him. But the more outstanding exception is Gerasim, a young peasant who is employed as the butler's assistant. Gerasim is cheerful, candid with Ivan Ilych about the fact that he is going to die, and displays a loving willingness to help the sick man and comfort him. Gerasim's candor and love seem to be connected with his own acceptance of mortality; it is as though he, alone of all the people in the house, sees that this matter of illness, humiliation, weakness, and death that Ivan Ilych is suffering is our common lot, a tie that binds us into a brotherhood. Gerasim sees that the bell tolls not just for Ivan Ilych, but for himself as well. So instead of fleeing to his own comforts and pleasures, Gerasim is drawn in compassion to the disgusting, helpless, dying Ivan Ilych. Ivan Ilych finds comfort in the presence of this strong, healthy young man, who sometimes sits through the night with Ivan Ilych's legs propped on his shoulders, because the dying man feels this eases his pain. "Health, strength, and vitality in other people were offensive to him, but Gerasim's strength and vitality did not mortify but soothed him" (p. 137). Gerasim's love is evidently an important factor in Ivan Ilych's "salvation."

The disease progresses, the loneliness deepens. The next stage in his "salvation" is that he begins to question his former life: " 'Maybe I did not live as I ought to have done,' it suddenly occurred to him. 'But how could that be, when I did everything properly?' he replied, and immediately dismissed from his mind this, the sole solution of all the riddles of life and death, as something quite impossible" (p. 148). Then he asks himself what he really wants. To live, and not to suffer, he answers. But how? And his mind is carried back in a survey of his life, and he finds that there is really little of it he would want to live again, except for some scenes in his childhood. All the rest has been so artificial, so much a matter of doing things and being something in order to please others, to get ahead, or establish superiority over others. There was so little genuine human *living* in it all. It begins to dawn on him that his life has *not* been proper, despite all its proprieties, and a suffering even greater than his physical sufferings comes over him: "His mental sufferings were due to the fact that that night, as he looked at Gerasim's sleepy, good-natured face with its prominent cheek-bones, the question suddenly occurred to him, 'What if my whole life has really been wrong?' " (p. 152). The next morning, when he sees one by one his footman, his wife, his daughter, and then the doctor, this conviction that he has missed life by overlaying it with trivialities, by exchanging it for things that are not life, is confirmed. For he sees in their deceitfulness and self-deceit, in their attitude that death belongs to Ivan Ilych and not to themselves, a reflection of himself; that is the way *he* lived, and it is the antithesis of life.

There ensues a struggle in Ivan Ilych's consciousness in which the issue is whether he will acknowledge the truth that he has missed the point of life. He feels that he is being thrust into a black sack, and he struggles against this, but at the same time feels that his greatest agony is that he cannot get right into it. The black sack is of course death, but now not physical death. It is *spiritual* death, the absolute renunciation of any claim to have lived life properly. The threat of physical death is what has brought him to this point of dying spiritually, but physical death is only a means to this greater and more important—indeed, all-important—death. Giving up his claim to "righteousness" is an agony all right, but he has got far enough in the process to see that his "righteousness" is the real burden on his soul, the thing that is *really* killing him. The real enemy is not physical death, but that ego which makes itself the center of the universe, turning other people into instruments and slaves, making claims of righteousness and immortality, and surrounding itself with illusions in the service of this great lie. So great an enemy is that ego that its death *is* life, and the prospect of physical death has brought Ivan Ilych to the point of seeing this truth.

Then something happens which carries him beyond merely *seeing* it. Outwardly he is screaming and flailing his arms about. One arm falls on the head of his young son, who clutches it and, weeping, kisses it:

> At that very moment Ivan Ilych fell through [into the black sack] and caught sight of the light, and it was revealed to him that though his life had not been what it should have been, this could still be rectified. He asked himself, "What *is* the right thing?" and grew still, listening. Then he felt that someone was kissing his hand. He opened his eyes, looked at his son, and felt sorry for him. His wife came up to him and he glanced at her. She was gazing at him open-mouthed, with un-dried tears on her nose and cheek and a despairing look on her face. He felt sorry for her too. (p. 155)

In this moment Ivan Ilych, almost for the first time since his childhood, *loves* another human being. He has died to that self which clung to its claims—of righteousness and of the right to live and to live on its own terms—and so is now able to be humanely conscious of his son and wife. The inexorable prospect of utter annihilation has caused every artificiality with which he has hidden life from himself to fall away, leaving him naked and stripped of every defense. And what he finds when all is stripped away is not nothing, as he had feared, but *himself*, the self which all these years he had betrayed and denied and safely jammed into oblivion by decorum: " 'And death . . . where is it?' He sought his former accustomed fear of death and did not find it. 'Where is it? What death?' There was no fear because there was no death. In place of death there was light. 'So that's what it is!' he exclaimed aloud. 'What joy!' " (pp. 155–156). Ivan Ilych remains in this state of joy for another two hours, and then dies.

IVAN Ilych dies contented, indeed joyful, despite having no notion at all of being delivered from the permanent annihilation of his consciousness. The joy he experiences in the last two hours of life does not stem from the hope of resurrection, but from a sense of being released from his insatiable, grasping, and haughty ego, which the prospect of annihilation has gradually caused him to feel as an intolerable burden. He has no more fear of extinction, not because it has been forestalled or short-circuited by belief in a life after death, but because the concern for continuation of life has been utterly submerged in a greater concern, which we might call the concern for authenticity. In a paradoxical turn of events, triviality, disingenuousness, and love-lessness, which seemed at first to be the acceptable order of the day, have become the hellish horror of horrors; while death, which at first seemed the ultimate enemy, has put on a mild face and a soft beckoning voice and become the savior.

In the remainder of this chapter I want to reflect on two objections to the suggestions I made in Chapter 3, objections of a sort that might very well lie behind Tolstoy's story as its ideological starting point. You will remember that my point was this: the Christian is called to live by hope, hope in the resurrection of the dead and the future kingdom of God, an eternal and righteous kingdom. In the mature Christian, who lives constantly in God's presence and by the hope of eternal life, the fear of death will have been rooted out. He conceives death not as annihilation, but as a passage to another life, or as a temporary sleep. But most of us Christians do not walk so wholly in the presence of God, and so trustingly mindful of his promises. We are doubting and worldly. Our hearts are where our treasure is, and our treasure, like Ivan Ilych's before his experience of release, is in this world; our little pleasures, our reputations, our wealth, our homes, our achievements and expertise. But the fact of death means that the person who puts his heart into such things is in despair. Only the person whose treasure is the eternal kingdom of God is free from despair. And so there is a sense in which, even in the Christian scheme of things, death can be a savior—a minor savior, or perhaps the Savior's helper. For the fact of death, if we realistically reckon with it, will draw Christians out of the world and set us on our way to the kingdom of God. For this reason we must not deny death in the many ways that come so naturally to us, but should cultivate a sense of our transience in this world—not out of morbidity, but for the sake of nurturing our passion for the eternal kingdom which God promises us in the gospel.

Now the high-minded people I mentioned at the beginning of this chapter will object to the Christian scheme not just because they believe there is no such thing as eternal life, but for what to their minds are much more important reasons. They will hold that the belief in eternal life—and thus also the Christian's edifying use of the prospect of death—is *morally degrading*, and this for two reasons. First, it is impossible to divorce the belief in heaven from a reward mentality, and a reward mentality is the very antithesis of an authentic and moral life. And second, the egocentrism which lies at the foundation of all moral failure is so deep and tenacious that nothing can save us from its misery short of looking straight in the teeth of unconditional obliteration, as Ivan Ilych was forced to do. In the next two sections, I want to examine these claims.

THE first objection goes something like this: the reason it is so difficult to assess the ethical value of an action is that the value lies not just in the observable action, much less in its consequences, but rather in its *motive*. Of course, there are cases in which a motive is obviously bad: a wealthy person writes a check for $100,000 to a charitable organization and then demands her money back when the society informs her that it is not their policy to publicize the names of donors. In this case the donor seems to have primarily desired not the humanitarian purposes of the organization but her own public glorification. Her desire was not a moral one, but a desire for a certain kind of reward. This is an obvious case, but many cases are more subtle than this. We sometimes wonder about even our own motive in doing some good deed: Was I just afraid I'd feel guilty if I didn't do it? Would I have done it if I had known that nobody would ever know about it? Did I do it primarily because I looked forward to the expressions of gratitude from my beneficiary? Or worse yet, did I do it to make myself feel superior to my beneficiary? And so on and on. The enormous difficulty of acting in a wholly moral way comes out when we begin to make the distinction between moral and nonmoral motives. Most of us don't even come close to passing the test most of the time. We are a lot like Ivan Ilych in his "prime."

But a great herd of philosophers in the last couple hundred years have taken this ordinary but very important distinction between moral and nonmoral motives and twisted it into something quite different. They say that considerations of advantage (what I have called more crudely "reward") and moral considerations belong to entirely different categories. And by this they mean that the desire for some advantage or reward can *never* be a moral desire. Immanuel Kant, the apparent father of this confusion, avers convincingly that a shopkeeper who for lucre's sake refrains from overcharging children is not by that token an honest man. He is moved not by honesty, but by avarice. But a couple of paragraphs later, exemplifying what to his mind is the same point, he tells us that humane actions are also without any genuine moral worth, insofar as they arise from the doer's concern for the happiness of others. We can tell for sure that a person's acts of benevolence have moral worth only if he is lacking the *desire* for another's happiness and acts merely as a matter of *duty*. Kant makes the same point with a distinction between practical love and pathological love. Pathological love is the kind we have for friends, family, and perhaps even strangers if we happen to *wish* for their welfare and *want* to do them good. Pathological love has no moral worth because, he suggests, in exercising it we are only fulfilling our own desires. We exemplify practical (i.e., moral) love when we do something good for someone not because we have any inclination to do it, but simply because it is our duty (see *Foundations of the Metaphysics of Morals*).

It is easy to see how this artificial and austere theory of moral psychology would lead to criticism of the Christian spirituality we are considering. In such a scheme of things the eternal kingdom for which the Christian hopes is seen as an "advantage," even a "reward," which cannot be achieved apart from moral purification. Thus if a person chooses his behavior and life-style in this life because he desires that life which is to come, then according to these thinkers such a person *cannot* be acting morally. Not only (so goes the objection) is the person acting out of a desire (like the individual who takes pleasure in relieving the suffering of others), he is even acting out of an *extrinsic* desire. For the person who simply enjoys seeing people relieved of their suffering, at least the object of pleasure is something closely connected with the benevolent act. But in the case of the Christian who acts in hope of the coming kingdom, the object of desire is something different, and distant, from the action itself. In doing acts of charity for the sake of heaven he is just like the shopkeeper who commits acts of fairness for the sake of money. (I should note that Kant himself did not use his theory of ethical motivation as an argument against believing in immortality; that inference has been added by others.)

This objection has two stages, and each is erroneous. First, the distinction between moral considerations and considerations of advantage is false when it is made absolute, as these philosophers make it. It is certainly true that *often*, when we act for our advantage, our actions are without moral worth. But is it always so? Do moral considerations and considerations of advantage never overlap? Obviously they do. For the person in whom justice has become a character trait rather than just a duty, seeing injustice will be a painful thing. He will *love* justice, *desire* it, and in its absence *long* for it. In the compassionate person the sight of a hungry or mistreated child will be cause for dissatisfaction. The moral life is a life of *passions*. The feeding of the hungry will be to the compassionate person as much a "reward" or "advantage" as the making of a lot of money will be to the avaricious person. To the just person the rectification of injustice will be a satisfaction of his personal longing. The more deeply a person develops the less important does the concept of duty become. We have duties only because we are *not* yet completely moral. The perfected saint feels no duties, only joys and sorrows. So these philosophers are wrong in thinking that desires and considerations of "advantage" are ruled out in the person who has truly become himself. And if this is so, why couldn't one of the moral person's desires, indeed the summation of all his deepest desires, be the kingdom of heaven?

The second stage of the objection is the claim that the desire for eternal life is even worse, morally, than other desires, because it is extrinsic to the moral life. In a book entitled *Death and Immortality*, which should really have been called *Death and Authenticity*, the British philosopher D. Z. Phillips says this:

> It has been seen that construing belief in the immortality of the soul as the final state which gives men good reasons for acting in certain ways now falsifies the character of moral regard. It certainly allows no room for anything that might be meant by the spirituality of the soul. It seems to me that if people lead a certain kind of life simply because of the final set of consequences to which it leads, they are indifferent to that way of life. (p. 30)

But this objection rests both on the Kantian mistake that I examined above, and a misconception of heaven, "the final state which gives men good reasons for acting." If you picture eternal life as a context of endless surfing, card playing, gin drinking, and coeducational hot-tubbing, and then figure that the way to get your hands on this jackpot vacation is to deny yourself, take up your cross, and embark upon a short but painful ministry to the headhunters of New Guinea, then I think Phillips's objection has fouled your eschatology. But in Christian thinking, surely, eternal life is the consummation and perfection of love to one's fellow personal creatures and of loving obedience to God. That is, it is the perfection of the moral life itself. It may include hot tubs and surfing, for all I know, but it is above all a context of obedience and love. So selfish people, people who have no compunction about acts of cruelty and injustice, people who want to live independently of God and be left to their own pleasures — such people cannot desire the kingdom of heaven as it is conceived by Christian faith. They may think they desire it, but they would find it a very unpleasant place to be if they somehow landed there. (See C. S. Lewis's *The Great Divorce* for an imaginative depiction of this situation.)

Phillips is wrong in thinking that leading a life of love is incompatible with believing that such a life leads to the immortal kingdom of God. The eternal kingdom *is* the "reward" of a spirit who has developed in such a way that such a kingdom can *look* like a reward to it. So it is the duty of every Christian to combat the worldliness in himself, to open himself to influences of holiness, and to practice those practices which will nurture him toward being the sort of person to whom the kingdom of heaven really looks like an advantage and a reward. But a life of growing moral sensitivity and toughness is, I think, more than just compatible with the hope of this reward. It is positively nourished and encouraged by this hope. It is very easy to get discouraged in the moral life; as soon as the going begins to get rough, one is tempted not just to violate the standards, but to lower them. The temptation is to say, "It can't be done; it is hopelessly idealistic. Justice and love are a dream dreamt of by youths and fanatics, but a grown man knows better; a little tinge of justice here and there, a hint of love, this is the most that one can or ought to expect. For the rest, let us enjoy ourselves. We must be realists." Against such dulling compromise, the resolute preaching of the kingdom of heaven can be a powerful antidote. It says, "Don't give up. Indeed, you'd *better* not give up. For God, who is in control of things, is going to make complete justice and perfect love the very structure of the world. In trimming down your moral vision, you're setting yourself at odds with the creator of heaven and earth."

T HE other moral argument against the Christian hope goes like this: because of the vanity of everything that man accomplishes under the sun, the only thing of real worth is something which does not show by the light of the sun — namely, the moral virtue of the individual human heart. But the systematic obstacle to every virtue is human selfishness, what Iris Murdoch calls "the fat relentless ego." Ambition, scorn, envy, greed, injustice, cruelty: the disease in every case is traceable to the same source — the self's nonnegotiable claim to be number one in the universe. The ego is a very hard nut to crack, so hard, in fact, that nothing short of confronting its absolute annihilation will bring it to the humility which is the foundation of all the virtues. In *The Sovereignty of Good*, Murdoch says,

> Goodness is connected with the acceptance of real death and real chance and real transience and only against the background of this acceptance, which is psychologically so difficult, can we understand the full extent of what virtue is like. The acceptance of death is an acceptance of our own nothingness which is an automatic spur to our concern with what is not ourselves. The good man is humble. . . . (p. 103)

Belief in immortality, therefore, is harmful to human beings, because it gives them an "out" from the only remedy which is radical enough to make them good.

I agree both that humility is central to human goodness, and that confronting death can foster it. Death levels. The most successful businessman, the most powerful politician, the most popular Hollywood star are, with respect to death, in the same boat as the poorest, most inept, and despised human being on earth. It is our duty, in honesty, to dwell on the shortness of our life. When we do, we find that the edge is taken off our worldly ambitions, our greed, our ruthlessness, our cruelty, our willingness to scorn and despise those who are less virtuous, wealthy, intelligent, or popular than we. A heartfelt reflection on our own death can be an ingredient in the pilgrimage to seeing every person we meet as our brother and sister.

But must the death which we confront be conceived as utter annihilation for it to have this effect? If the only way to conceive the afterlife were as a continuation of the present order of things, in which the rule is dog-eat-dog for the survival of the ego, then perhaps so. But I have suggested in the last section that this is not the only way of conceiving it, and indeed is very far from the Christian view. Heaven is a context (with some distant analogies on earth, I might add) in which those people whose fat relentless egos have not been killed will be extremely uncomfortable. For most of us, looking forward to this kind of afterlife is itself a kind of death, and can have the same humbling effect as the prospect of physical death.

But I would like to assert too that death, whether it is understood as utter annihilation or as the passageway to "judgment," is not the only, and maybe not even the chief, way that people are freed from themselves and empowered to live in selfless obedience to God or love of their fellow creatures. Perhaps the most powerful solvent of the self-encased self is the relentless love of another for it. "We love because He first loved us," says the apostle. In the face of the irresistible affirmation of oneself by a lover, it becomes almost impossible not to open up and forget oneself in responsive love. There is nothing that drives us more deeply into egoism than the feeling that if we don't look out for ourselves, no one else will. Even the most humble can sometimes be tempted into self-assertion by the relentless assaults upon him of a social environment in which each person is thought to have to establish his or her worth at the expense of others. And when, into such a context, there breaks a person who accepts another not according to these standards, but in love, she enters as a liberating ray of grace into a world of darkness, casting down the other's defenses, and lighting up his neighbors in his eyes. The story of Ivan Ilych's transformation would be implausible without the roles played by Gerasim and Ivan Ilych's young son. Even Tolstoy could not convince us, I think, that the confrontation with death *alone* could make a loving, self-abandoning person of Ivan Ilych.

In the present world, liberating experiences of love are rare. Here egoism is the formula for survival. It is a world in which most commodities and social positions and personal qualities are prized *because* not everybody can have them, and so they engender in those who lack them envy and in their possessors pride. And the envious and prideful fuel one another's sin and harden the encasement around each which prevents them from communion. But in the new world to which Christians look forward, all these pressures that foster the entrenchment of the fat relentless ego, all these encouragements to selfishness and lovelessness, will be gone, and in their place will be an over-powering presence of love. What Ivan Ilych experienced in a small but powerful way in the person of Gerasim, the less-than-perfect individual entering heaven will experience as irresistible grace. Love is just as irresistible as death, with one proviso — that the individual to whom love is offered not be *completely* without love himself. For I suppose that if one is *entirely* self-enclosed, has no sensitivity *at all* to the claims of other persons on him, but treats them merely and always as means to his own private ends, then even the love of God and of all the saints in heaven will not be able to transform him. Ivan Ilych's suscep-tibility to be changed by the love of Gerasim shows that he was not beyond redemption. So it seems to me that it is a faulty psychology or a lack of imagination or both which lie at the basis of the claim that only the confrontation with absolute death is capable of making a person completely good.

But beyond this, there is a certain absurdity in the position of Murdoch. She tells us, heroically, "a genuine sense of mor-tality enables us to see virtue as the only thing of worth" (p. 99).

But if virtue is the only thing of worth, and if "real death and real chance and real transience" (p. 103) must be believed if we are to come to this realization, then there is not even a grain of truth in the intuitions we have explored in Chapter 3. The perception of death as an enemy is entirely mistaken, according to Murdoch, and is completely due to the fat relentless ego. Only insofar as we are selfish, immoral, and unfulfilled do we perceive death as an enemy. The truth is not, as Christianity holds, that death is both an enemy and a friend. It is simply that the prospect of death, in the sense of utter annihilation, is the best and only real friend a person ever had. It is the necessary condition of his fulfillment as a human being.

But there is something outrageous about making virtue "the only thing of worth" and at the same time holding that the universe is so constituted that those beings in whom virtue is possible (and occasionally actual) flourish for a while and then sink into oblivion. Virtue, here, is conceived (rightly) as loving other people. But if absolute death is not only *my* destiny but also the destiny of those people who are the object of my virtue, is there not something deeply sad about virtue itself? I am not saying that there is anything like a logical contradiction here, but a contradiction rather of how, in our heart of hearts, we must feel that things ought to be. There is something offensive, something fundamentally shocking about a universe in which a being capable of love is allowed to be annihilated.

Let me put the matter another way. The love of virtue would seem to imply the love of life, since a dead person is not capable of virtue. So it would seem that even for Murdoch, who believes that virtue cannot be achieved apart from believing that one is confronted with absolute death, it would be preferable if we were not in fact destined to it. That is, the ideal situation would be one of deceit: the situation in which we all believe that we are going to be obliterated, but in fact we are going to live on to exercise our virtue. Or, to put it another way, Murdoch cannot really believe that virtue is the only thing of worth. She must believe that life too is of worth, even if it is worthless without virtue.

The Christian does not believe that virtue is the only thing of worth; of worth also is the life which is the only context in which virtue can be exercised: a conscious life of fellowship with God and man. And so for the Christian (as, I think, for non-Christians, if they could be brought to admit it), it would be an inexpressible pity if death were the eternal annihilation of the self. The reason is that if it is, it is also the annihilation of virtue; that is, it is the annihilation of a child of God. It is natural for us to grieve on the occasion of death, and more so if we are without hope. But it seems to me that if Murdoch is right, we have here a transformed and deepened sadness, the gloomiest and most incongruous of pictures. It is not now the screaming protest of the fat relentless ego against the ultimate threat to its godhead, but instead the quiet grief of love at the prospect that something as precious as a child of God should be lost in oblivion. And now I want to admit to a certain thinness in the feelings I described in Chapter 3. There is much in those feelings of the screaming protest of the fat relentless ego. But I think there is something else too, which prefigures the Christian apprehension. And that is the sense that in absolute death something of infinite value is slated to be snuffed out.

So Wittgenstein's suggestion that the "riddle" of death is completely submerged in the "riddle" of our unworthiness is not right. Death remains a "riddle," an incongruity and an embarrassment upon the face of the universe, unless it is conquered, as Christians believe it has been. But Wittgenstein's emphasis is right, even if his declaration is not. For Christians, inextricably tied up with the fact of death and the hope of life is the passion for moral worthiness, the hungering and thirsting for righteousness.

In this chapter and the last I have attempted to say a little about the foundation of the Christian emotions, a passion we might call the heart's seeking for the kingdom of God. My account has been progressive, in that the present chapter has approximated more nearly the description of Christian maturity than the previous one. In the previous chapter I described an embryonic passion for the kingdom of God, the yearning for a life beyond this finite existence, and defended it against some obvious objections. Then in the present chapter, in the course of answering a profound moral objection to the desire for eternal life, our understanding of this passion deepened and took on the second major aspect of correspondence to the Christian gospel: just as

Christianity is a message about God's triumph for us over the twin evils of sin and death, so the Christian's passion must be not only a desire for life-despite-death but also a desire for righteousness. For the life that is offered us is *essentially* a moral life, one of love for God and neighbor; in the Christian conception of the kingdom, the living and the being worthy are not separable. In the next chapter I shall attempt to increase our understanding of the Christian passion still further by beginning to look *inside* the moral life. If I succeed, the account will perhaps give a yet deeper insight into the passion basic to the Christian emotions: an overriding enthusiasm for the life of perfect fellowship with God and neighbor in the promised kingdom.

I shall focus my discussion on humility both because of its great intrinsic interest as a virtue of the Christian life and also as a way of making clear the connection between moral striving and Christian spirituality. My concentrating on humility does not suggest that this is the only virtue worth striving for (though I do think it very basic to the Christian outlook); it is, for our present purpose, an example. I hope to show that moral striving is both an essential part of spiritual growth (that is, spiritual growth *is* moral growth) and a ground of self-despair which sensitizes the individual to the grace of Jesus Christ. The more serious you become about attaining moral goodness, the more serious you have become about God's kingdom. And the more actively you get involved in the endeavor to straighten yourself out morally, the more deeply do you perceive the grace of Jesus as food for your spirit.

✳ 5 ✳
Humility as a Moral Project

HUMILITY is a much maligned virtue. Even in the minds of Christians who believe, because Christ says so, that the meek are blessed, there is sometimes an uneasiness about humility. It seems so often unrealistic, impractical, or downright demeaning—not a *virtue* at all. I think this uneasiness can be largely traced to the sway of worldly ways of thinking. We find humility repugnant because it conflicts with the deepest of our personal values—even if it accords nicely with our *spoken* ones. It is deep in us to conceive ourselves in terms of power over others; we are convinced that the pursuit of self-esteem is the same as the pursuit of advantageous comparison with our fellows. We are committed to building our egos on a foundation of inferiority—the inferiority of others.

But our distaste for humility can also be traced to one or more confusions about what humility is. So I want to clarify the concept of humility as a virtue, and to begin by distinguishing it from some things which are clearly *not* virtues, and with which it is often confused.

First, there is the case of Uriah Heep, a character in Charles Dickens's *David Copperfield*:

> Father and me was both brought up at a foundation school for boys. . . . They taught us all a deal of umbleness—not much else that I know of, from morning to night. We was to be umble to this person, and umble to that; and to pull off our caps here, and to make bows there; and always to know our place, and abase ourselves before our betters. And we had such a lot of betters! Father got the monitor-medal by being umble. So did I. Father got made sexton by being umble. He had the character, among the gentlefolks, of being such a well-behaved man, that they were determined to bring

him in. 'Be umble, Uriah,' says father to me, 'and you'll
get on. . . . Be umble,' says father, 'and you'll do!' And
really it ain't done bad! . . . I got to know what umbleness did, and I took to it. I ate umble pie with an
appetite. . . . 'People like to be above you,' says father;
'keep yourself down.' I am very umble to the present
moment, Master Copperfield, but I've got a little power!
(pp. 604– 605)

Umbleness, as Uriah Heep practices it, is a means of getting
ahead in the world. It is a pattern of deferential and self-de-
meaning behavior calculated to play upon other people's sense
of self-importance, thereby procuring for its practitioner ad-
vancement in rank, medals and honors, and suchlike. Umbleness
is no more (indeed it is less) a moral virtue than good looks or
a deep voice or having friends in high places. It is compatible
with attitudes quite contrary to humility. The hostage of a ter-
rorist may practice umbleness with his captor as a means of
"getting on," all the while despising him as the very scum of the
earth. And surely the desire to beat out all the other servants in
the contest for the monitor-medal is the very opposite of humility. We can feel contempt for the attitude of Uriah Heep
without feeling it for humility.

Uriah Heep's umbleness is not a very subtle deception. But
there is a subtler form of the same thing, which the philosopher
Friedrich Nietzsche is famous for having noted. He pointed out
that what seems like humility is often (he thought always) mo-
tivated down deep by the desire to topple people who are
stronger, or more intelligent, or higher in rank from their positions of strength. "Humility" is a strategic device used by the
weak in the competition for ascendancy over other human beings.
If a person (or group) finds that he cannot compete successfully
in terms of worldly success, he does what he can to change the
terms of competition to something in which he *can* succeed.
And the perverse genius of the "slave morality," as Nietzsche
calls it, is to make a virtue of failure (namely weakness, lowliness, degradation) and a failure of what is naturally a virtue
(namely success, power, intelligence, nobility, haughtiness, fla-
grant self-approval). Thus the losers and misfits of the world try
to become winners by convincing everybody that losing is really
winning. Then those who have worldly success will see that it

is not so great after all—indeed it is pride, selfishness, callousness, and other vices—while people who think themselves meek and lowly sinners undeserving of what little they have are the good people, and noble characters, the *real* winners in the game of life. Blessed are the meek, for by their strategic weakness they will wrest the reins of power from the great and inherit the earth. So, according to Nietzsche, there is at the root of all humility a very unhumble motive: the desire to rank oneself superior by putting down the mighty from their thrones and exalting those of low degree.

(I should note that what Nietzsche finds despicable about humility is not that it is an effort to establish one's superiority over others. For him, that is a natural, inevitable disposition of the human heart, and not at all to be despised in itself. In the noble and powerful ones who recognize glory in themselves and have no compunction about asserting it, this predilection for superiority is a natural and innocent attitude. Humility is despicable not because it is unhumble, but because it is a reversal of true values, a lie in which what is really bad [lowly, degraded, weak, sickly] is made out to be good.)

Nietzsche seems to think that humility always is and must be (presumably because of human nature) merely "humility"—self-abasement deceitfully aimed at self-exaltation. He seems to leave out the possibility that people might abdicate the power play model of life altogether, getting their self-esteem some other way than by parasitically deriving it from their power over others. If we believe that it is possible—even in part—for us to free ourselves from the competition for power and if we believe that this way of viewing life is intrinsically evil, then we will want to resist Nietzsche on this point and hold out for both a better conception of humility and for the possibility of realizing it. But we must also admit the justice of his analysis as a criticism of much that passes for humility. Much of it *is* the despicable device he says it is. We, like Uriah Heep but with greater self-deceit and greater psychological sophistication, do in many subtle ways debase ourselves to establish our ascendancy over others or to protect ourselves in a competition for power that we are very reluctant to lose. Our "humility" has the double defect of deceitfulness and pride. Nietzsche's is a deep criticism of many people whose moral life is outwardly Christian (and of many who have no interest in Christianity).

T HIS virtue is also confused with low self-esteem, submissiveness to other persons, or seeing oneself as inferior to others. Unlike the confusion of humility with umbleness, this confusion does not necessarily involve deceit, nor make of humility a device for getting something. It can be a perfectly honest (though pitiable) self-assessment, and nothing more. William Mac-Dougall's view is typical. Humility, he says,

> may be due to the original strength of the submissive tendency, or may be the result of much chastening, of rebuffs and failures which gradually induce in a man a lowly estimate of his qualities and weaken, by repeated discouragement, the self-assertive impulse. (*Character and the Conduct of Life,* p. 129)

The picture here is that of a person limited by genetics or beaten down by failure. He does not have much confidence in his own abilities and judgments. He does not initiate projects and human relationships. He would rather follow orders than give them, would rather have others make the decisions in his life. His failures (or his genes) have rendered him a psychologically passive personality, a Mr. Milquetoast who does not object to being told where to sit and wait, or even to being utilized as a convenient wiping-place for muddy feet. Anyone who undertook to cultivate this disposition in his children would be doing them a momentous disservice. This is not humility, but rather a deeply engrained and ramified humiliation. Humility, by contrast, is not incompatible with aggressiveness, self-confidence, and a high view of one's own abilities; indeed, as I shall soon argue, it is a transcendent form of self-confidence.

Sad to say, Christians have indulged—indeed reveled—in this confusion about humility. Instances abound in mystical and ascetic Christian literature of the view that the truly humble person sees himself unfavorably in comparison with his fellows and incapable of anything good. Typical are the following remarks from Walter Hilton's *The Stairway of Perfection* (a mystical treatise of the fourteenth century):

> First of all, this is how you must practice meekness. You must judge yourself in your will (and in your feelings,

if you can manage it) to be unable to dwell among men and unworthy to serve God in conversation with His servants. Further, you must consider yourself unprofitable to your fellow-Christians, lacking both the intelligence and the strength to perform the good works of the active life and help your fellow-Christians as other men and women do. . . . You shall judge yourself more foul and more wretched than any creature alive, so that you'll hardly be able to ~~put~~ up with yourself for the greatness and number of your sins and the filth that you'll experience in yourself. (pp. 80, 81)

There are several reasons why we must reject this picture. First, it seems to make sin a prerequisite of humility; if this is the case, then the goodness of perfected saints disqualifies them for this virtue. But humility—like love and unlike hope—seems to be a virtue that you can have in heaven. Second, if everybody who is humble has to believe that he is lacking both the intelligence and strength to do good works as other men and women do, then it would seem that not everybody's humility can be based on a true belief. But it doesn't seem fair to make a virtue such that to have it some people have to believe a falsehood about themselves. What about the unfortunate people who excel in the intelligence and strength to do good works? They seem to be condemned to choose between humility and truth. And third, this conception of humility requires that the individual indulge in precisely that activity which so easily slides into pride—the building of one's view of oneself on a foundation of comparison with others. Unlike the straightforwardly proud person, he does not seek a *flattering* comparison with others. And yet the humility he achieves by this means he still achieves, in a sense, at somebody else's expense; for if it is true that he is more wretched than any creature alive, then no other creature is going to be in quite such an advantageous position for cultivating the virtue. Humility, strangely, turns out to be an elitist virtue.

It would be better to try to conceive of humility as a matter of viewing everybody as ultimately or basically *equal*. The belief in people's ultimate equality will probably have to be one which transcends appearances, since from all that is obvious people are so unequal. But if such a belief can be integrated into a person's emotional life, it will allow humility to be compatible with people's believing the truth about themselves, and also allow them to eschew the whole dangerous business of building self-assessments on watching to see how they're doing in comparison with others. Such a view would not have to deny obvious individual differences of beauty, ability, and virtue, since its conception of human equality would turn on a feature of the self which transcends such differences.

"Humility" comes from *humus*, Latin for earth. This origin of the word might suggest that being humble is being "down to earth," not trying to be "up in the clouds" where one doesn't belong. It need not mean groveling in the dirt while others are standing erect and dignified; it might mean being solidly a member of the earthy human family by not trying to opt out of it upwardly (and in fact, by God's standard, opting out of it downwardly, ending one's endeavor to be more than a member of the family by becoming less).

I want to suggest that the opposite of humility as a virtue is not self-confidence, initiative, assertiveness, and self-esteem, but instead pushiness, scorn of "inferiors," rejoicing in the downfall of others, envy, resentment and grudge bearing, ruthless ambition, haughtiness, shame at failure or disadvantageous comparison, and the need to excel others to think well of oneself. Humility is the ability, without prejudice to one's self-esteem, to admit one's inferiority, in this or that respect, to another. And it is the ability, without increment to one's self-esteem or prejudice to the quality of one's relationship with another, to remark one's superiority, in this or that respect, to another. As such, humility is a psychological principle of independence from others and a necessary ground of genuine fellowship with them, an emotional independence of one's judgments concerning how one ranks vis-a-vis other human beings. It is perhaps an aspect of what Kierkegaard called being an "individual." Next I want to reflect on the idea of a *spiritual* relationship and show that humility is necessary for such relationships.

MOST of my associations with people are largely instrumental and external. By "instrumental" I mean that I relate to the other person for some other purpose than fellowship with him or her. Most of the personal relationships of our daily lives have the purpose of making money, of getting some job done, of acquiring some good or other, etc. To say that a relationship is largely instrumental is not to say that it is wholly so. My engagement as a teacher with students is largely aimed at getting a job done — namely, teaching them something. Yet part of what motivates me to stick with the teaching profession may be the friendships that I enjoy with my students. By "external" I mean that I relate to others by conventions, by behavior that is judged proper or improper without regard to my motives or attitudes. Thus in hiring someone to mow my lawn, I am thought to have been impeccably decent if I treat her respectfully and pay her a fair wage. The question of the "propriety" of my thoughts about her doesn't arise (or so it seems) even if, for example, I take a mild, fleeting joy in the fact that she is having financial troubles or silently rejoice in how advantageously my own daughter compares to her in beauty and intelligence. My relationship to her may seem to me entirely instrumental and external, that is, entirely without a spiritual dimension. After all, I just want to get the lawn mowed. If I am a Christian, then of course I do not believe that any of my relationships can be merely instrumental and external. I am called upon to *love* my neighbor. And yet even Christians fall into thinking in purely instrumental and external terms; this is, in a way, natural, for most of our interaction with others *is* for the purpose of getting some job done or for some other external purpose.

But even the non-Christian, who may think it entirely proper for some of his relationships to be merely instrumental, will have to admit that the most significant ones in his life are not. These are relationships of friendship and love, ones whose *point* is fellowship, and whose *substance* is attitudes fundamental to fellowship. The young woman who mows my lawn may say, "I don't care what he thinks about me, just as long as he pays me," but my daughter cannot say, "I don't care what Papa thinks of me, as long as he's a good father to me." And my best friend can't say, "I don't care what attitudes Roberts takes towards me, just as long as he remains a good friend." I demand not just loving *behavior* from my lover, but a certain enthusiasm for my person, a heartfelt devotion, a tendency to rejoice and grieve with me at appropriate moments, a deep respect. Here, the attitudes of the parties to the relationship are its very substance, and this is why a lack of humility is destructive to a person's spiritual life: it subverts his spiritual relationships, the deepest and most important relationships of his life. Pride cuts a person off from fellowship with others. It isolates him and, however little he may recognize the fact, degrades him. He who exalts himself will be humbled.

Pride is most likely to manifest itself in relationships in which the two individuals are close enough to equality in worldly terms to feel themselves competitors, and yet are not very close friends or lovers. The most famous and brilliant philosopher in America is not likely to get much satisfaction when his analytic ability is considered superior to that of a graduate student from Western Kentucky University, but he may get intense satisfaction from contemplating his superiority to another member of the Harvard philosophy faculty. (He may, in fact, feel himself less alienated from, and be less alienating to, the graduate student than the colleague.) Similarly the graduate student from WKU is less likely to feel malicious envy of the brilliant philosopher than the philosopher's colleagues are, since she is not even in the running so to speak. If the WKU student feels envious of anybody's philosophic abilities, it is more likely to be those of some fellow graduate student.

On the other hand, the symptoms of pride (such as envy, superciliousness, putdowns, condescension, scorn) may be absent between two persons who are "in the running" with one another if the two are very close friends or lovers. This is possible if they "identify" with each other. The superior one does not nourish his ego from his superiority to the other, because this person is almost an extension of himself. (Just as he would not take malicious pride in the fact that he is a better mathematician today than he was ten years ago, because he "identifies" with the self that he was ten years ago.) Similarly the inferior one does not take offense against the superior, envying and hating him for the degradation he feels at being rendered inferior by the comparison, because he identifies with the superior one. Indeed, he can take a sort of pride in the other's superiority, because he feels that the other is part of himself. A wife, traditionally, has seen the achievements of her husband in this way: even if she herself is "in the running," she doesn't succumb to envy of her husband, but instead takes pride over others in his superiority; his ascendancy over others *is* hers through identification. (Most wives in this situation in our time probably have "mixed feelings": they are proud to be associated with their hotshot husband, but at the same time envious of his ascendancy.)

It is not difficult to feel why people who lack humility are spiritually bankrupt. Their capacity for human relationships — the spiritual ones which are the most important of their lives — is poisoned by the tendency to climb to eminence at someone else's expense. The proud person is one who needs to have some-body who compares disadvantageously with himself before he will feel good about himself. He says to himself, "I may be stupid and ugly, but all is not lost; compared to a guy I know in Mrs. Foster's rooming house, I'm a combination of Albert Einstein and Robert Redford." Or perhaps he says "I am the greatest." But in either case it is the comparison that builds the self, so there is always another person, somewhere in the background at least, who is supporting the weight of my ego with the suffering of his failure to make the grade relative to me.

Now you may object: "First, you said relationships of fellowship and love are the important, the spiritual ones. Then you observed that the proud individual gets his self-confidence by comparing himself with others who are less advantaged than he. But your conclusion, to the effect that pride ruins the most important relationships, does not follow from these two observations. That would follow only if the *same* people upon whose shoulders of weakness you construct your glory were the people with whom you are purporting to have these important relationships. But that needn't be the case. Indeed, you tend to build your friendships with people who are your equals, and not therefore very good candidates to become, by their wretchedness, the cornerstone of your self-esteem. So I don't see how these important relationships are spoiled by pride."

I will admit that the parasite strategy of the proud person's bid for self-esteem is not as obviously directed to his close friends as it is to the others about whom he *and* his close friend invidiously gossip. People who are clearly beyond the pale make good candidates, in one way, for pride fodder, because they do not offer serious competition with us. But in another way they are very inferior pride fodder, because being superior to them doesn't count nearly as heavily in ego-building as superiority to someone

roughly equal to you in whatever matter is the basis for comparison. So your closest friends are likely to be precisely the
kind of people whose inferiority holds out the greatest promise
of serving to build your pride. Their being your friends, and not
merely your rivals, means that you have come to some kind of
"understanding" with them in the matter of superiority/
inferiority.

Perhaps you play the role of acknowledged inferior and your
friend that of superior. You find this understanding acceptable,
perhaps because your very association with him enhances your
superiority to some other person or group. But now, ask yourself: what if suddenly you were promoted to a position of prom-
inence and power in the company, and in the eyes of the world
you had clearly established your superiority over him? If you are
a proud person, it is likely that the superciliousness which you
once directed to other inferiors will now be turned directly on
your "friend." That is, you will begin to rejoice in your superiority to *him*; *he* will become now the fodder for your pride.
Perhaps you will not admit this to yourself; perhaps you exercise, in the name of the spiritual relationship, a certain chaste
self-deception. But still, down in your heart, you know it feels
very good to have one-upped the old boy and reversed the roles.
What this sort of imagined case seems to say is that pride makes
a person ready to eat his "friends"; it gives one's "friendships"
a very unstable character, for given a slight shift in the circumstances, suddenly the "friend," who was *not* fodder for one's
pride, becomes such.

Or let us say that, in the "friendship," the understanding
which you two had was that *you* were the one in ascendancy,
and he was the acknowledged inferior. And now let it again
happen that the roles are reversed by some circumstance. Maybe
you don't admit to yourself that your self-esteem was invested
in being the big brother in that relation, the one to whom your
"friend" would come for advice, looking up in admiration. After
all, you do have a dim sense that this is a spiritual relationship,
and that your parasitically feeding on his inferiority is not good
for it. But now he has been catapulted to fame, and you are left
in relative obscurity. Will your relationship go on undisturbed?
Not, I think, if you are a proud person. Your reaction, instead,
will be envy, that is, a certain hatred of your "friend" now that

he has usurped your place and "put you down." Of course you may try to hide this, from him and from yourself. But still, that love has been poisoned. And my point is that what seemed to be love was already spoiled by your pride. It was not your "friend's" sudden rise to fame that spoiled everything; the relationship was spoiled already because pride was its foundation. Or, if pride was not precisely the foundation of the relationship, it was at any rate such a potent moving force in your self-understanding that the "friendship" was weak by comparison, like a soap bubble that will pop at the first thing that gets in its way.

It is not possible to be close friends with an unrepentant cannibal. Even if he is not at the moment eyeing my musculature with a fond view to the tenderloins, still the fact that my tenderloins are the *kind* of thing on which he feeds is going to spoil everything. I may not notice that the relationship is spoiled, of course. For one thing, I may be so crass that I accept this mutual cannibalism with equanimity; perhaps I don't have an inkling what spiritual friendship is. Dog-eat-dog is just the name of the game; what does it matter if after we've had some nice meals together, one of us ends up in the other's pot? Only I'd better watch out that if that happens, it's *me* who makes a meal of *him,* and not the other way around. On the other hand, if I am not so crass, I may achieve equanimity by deceiving myself a little about the mutual cannibalism. I say to myself, "I would never eat *him,* for he is my friend; and I'm sure he wouldn't eat me, either. It would never come to that. No, I'm sure it wouldn't." But the way to avoid all these troubles is, of course, to give up cannibalism.

Pride does spoil our spiritual relationships, even before it makes its overt appearance. It is an infection in the attitudes which make up the spiritual relationships. The infection may become an open symptom only when precipitated by some outward circumstance, but still it was a weakness present from the beginning.

Humility is the disposition gladly to construe as my equal every person who is presented to me. It is the disposition not to be touched in my self-esteem by the fact that someone is clearly ahead of me in the games of the world nor to find any satisfaction in noting that I am ahead of someone in those games. It is

the ability to have my self-esteem quite apart from any question
about my place in the social pecking order (whether the criterion
is accomplishments, education, beauty, money, power, fame, or
position); it is the loss of my spiritually cannibalistic appetite.
Humility is thus a deep self-confidence, running far deeper than
the tenuous self-confidence of the person who believes in himself
because there are others who look up to him.

If this is humility, two things follow. First, if adults are to
cultivate it, we need some way of conceiving of ourselves and
our neighbors jointly, by which they will appear to us as equals.
If we have no other way of "seeing" our neighbors than in terms
of the competitive games the world plays, we have little hope of
becoming humble. Our inclination to succumb to invidious comparisons is so great and the means of making these comparisons
are so readily available that a necessary part of our defense
against spiritual cannibalism will be an equally clear concep-
tualization of our neighbor as our equal. And second, we need
some basis of self-esteem other than our success in competition
with others. We cannot escape the need to believe ourselves
valuable, nor would we want to lose that capacity if we could.
To believe ourselves worthless is a terrible and unchristian thing;
and not to care that we are worthless is perhaps more woeful
still.

Christianity offers to satisfy both these conditions, and this
is a psychological recommendation for it. I do not deny that
there are other philosophies or world views which may satisfy
these conditions. For example, Kant's philosophy tells us that
rational beings must always be regarded not merely as means to
ends, but as ends in themselves. The Stoic philosophy tends to
see all persons as equal in that their circumstances (in terms of
which the inequalities are so obvious) are not the source of
peace; instead, the source of peace is an inner renunciation of
which all perhaps are (initially) equally capable. Existentialism
sees death as the Great Equalizer, and thus the basis of a kind
of humility (see Chapter 4).

But we are concerned with Christian spirituality, and Christianity is eminently well qualified to engender the evenhanded,
deep self-confidence which it names "humility." For it challenges
us to see every person as a brother or sister whom God so loved
that he humbled himself to death on a cross to reconcile us with

himself. The equality in terms of which a Christian is equipped to see every other is not that of inalienable rights (see the Declaration of Independence), of rationalness (see Kant), of the potential for resignation (see Stoicism), or of mortality (see existentialism). It is that they are all equally the objects of God's unspeakable love, all equally children (or potential children) of his household, members of his kingdom. The Christian's self-understanding is that she is precious before God—however much a sinner, however much a failure (or success) she may be by the standards of worldly comparisons—and that every other person she meets has the same status.

Now we can see that this vision is not only one that levels every distinction by which egos seek a glory which really demeans them. This vision, when appropriated, is also the ultimate ground of self-confidence. For the message is that God loves me for myself—not for anything I have achieved, not for my beauty or intelligence or righteousness or for any other "qualification," but simply in the way that a good mother loves the fruit of her womb. If I can get *that* into my head—or better, into my heart—then I won't be grasping desperately for self-esteem at the expense of others, and cutting myself off from my proper destiny, which is spiritual fellowship with them.

Anyone who has had a normal upbringing has some psychological basis for humility, however much he may have neglected it for a worldly understanding of himself. That basis is the love he has received in his childhood (and any genuine love he has received since then). Unless a parent is perverse indeed, her child will sense that he is treasured simply for himself. In countless ways, and usually without words, this love is communicated. But an explicit model is this: She looks into his eyes and says "I love you, Nathan," not because she always wanted a boy and he is a boy, nor because he has just picked up his toys, nor still less because he aced out the other kids in the coloring contest, but quite "out of the blue." Thus he grows, feeding his soul daily on an unconditional affirmation of his value. This implicit and inarticulate sense of his own worth, if it were carried into adulthood by becoming articulated in a definite life view, would be the radical self-confidence which Christians call humility: a self-confidence so deep, a personal integration so strong, that all comparison with other people, both advantageous and disadvantageous, slides off him like water off a duck's back, And this, it seems to me, is the psychological structure of the kingdom of heaven. Heaven is that society in which each member is so surrounded by and conscious of focused love—both the love of his God and of his fellow creatures—that inequalities of various sorts fade into a background of inattention. Competitiveness, other than of the most unserious and playful sort, ceases; superiority and inferiority in every respect cease to touch anyone's self-esteem.

Of course, people experience in their childhood varying amounts and qualities of this analogy to the kingdom of heaven. Some people have been more or less systematically taught, by their unbringing, that their worth *is* conditional upon their acing out the competition. They have experienced love being withheld from them when they performed badly, or were naughty, or came in second in the race. No upbringing could be better calculated to produce a spiritual cannibal, for two reasons: first, it has been ingrained in her mind that the way to self-value is the achievement of comparative excellence; and second, the deeper sense of self-worth which a person must have if she is to give up invidious ego building has not been established. In the extreme case of a perverting and depriving unbringing, the person has been so damaged that she cannot be held responsible for her perversity. She is like a person who has been trained to think that stealing is normal and then so deprived of the opportunity to get food by respectable means that she has no choice but to live by theft or starve. Even if an inkling descends upon her mind that stealing is wrong, she can hardly be much condemned if she chooses not to starve. In building our self-esteem at others' expense, we are all a *little* like the starving woman who violates another's property in order to survive. We are all socially damaged beings. But to the extent that we have known love, precisely to that extent can we be held responsible for our gluttonous, destructive, and ill-considered policy of building our self-esteem at the cost of fellowship.

No one is inducted into heaven on the strength of his parents' love. Those of us who have known love well enough to see that dog-eat-dog is a degradation of the spirit have, in participating in it, responsibly violated a trust. God has created us for fellowship with one another, and we have chosen instead to forsake it for something unsatisfying and despicable. Despite our parents' love, not one of us is humble, not one is innocent of the crime of spiritual cannibalism.

The church is a society of people who have undertaken the struggle to love one another with a spiritual love. They teach one another, week in and week out, the beauty and the duty of humility. They cultivate themselves and one another in the consciousness of the calling to perfect fellowship, and in responsibility before God they struggle against the evil that is in their hearts. The gospel has taught them they are children of God, and the fittingness of that conception for their deepest social needs has not been lost on them. So they struggle to view one another not as competitors, but instead as brothers and sisters all equally beloved of the Father, all equally and graciously bestowed with membership in his family.

The picture sketched in the preceding paragraph may have a ring of unfamiliarity. It doesn't sound much like any church I ever attended. But then the church I sketched isn't anything a person would "attend"; instead, it is a provisional, struggling foretaste of the kingdom of God, a little group of persons who have been touched by the vision of the kingdom included in the gospel of Jesus Christ. And many Christians may be familiar with *this* church, though probably only with fleeting instances of it. At any rate, it is within such a church that the struggle for humility is most likely to be undertaken in all seriousness.

But our question now is, What happens when humility is seriously accepted as a moral project? What happens, over the years, to the heart and understanding of one who reflects on the brother- and sisterhood of believers, and tries in the light of this to become humble? (For we are not speaking here of the Average Presbyterian, for whom the church is far from anything so momentous as a foretaste of the kingdom of God—who, indeed, is not acquainted with the church, though he knows by regular participation about the baptisms and organ music and potlucks that go on at the church.)

What happens is this: to the extent that I agree with the worldly cannibalistic attitude toward others, I will just accept it as "normal." But as I become more ethically sensitive, this complacency changes into a growing discontent with my attitudes. When I feel envious toward another, or experience a passing scorn for one who is "below" me, or take delight in a certain person's failure, I no longer give myself wholeheartedly to the attitude, but learn a kind of disgust for it and for myself. And now, if I believe that *God's* intention is that I should be a member of his kingdom and rejoice in every brother and sister who likewise and equally are members of it; and if I believe that my spiritual cannibalism is a degrading and hateful thing, a ruining of the perfect fellowship which God intends for me; then I shall become all the more concerned to eradicate it from my heart. And the more I participate in the life of the church (in the above defined sense), the more precious and desirable does this state of fellowship appear to me and the more horrible my own complicity in preventing it. Thus the ethical struggle begets a deepening of my passion for the kingdom of God. But it is a universal testimony of the saints that the more enthusiastic they become for the things of the Spirit, the more deeply aware they become of the evil in their hearts, until at last they *experience* what Christian thinkers have called bondage to sin. They come to realize that the *struggle* is hopeless, and that hope, if there is hope, must reside in some *rescue* operation. At this point of spiritual awareness, the individual is at a maximum of desire for the kingdom of God, and simultaneously at a minimum of his confidence to gain it by struggle.

But in the possession of that very same church which struggles for a spiritual love that is rightness before God is the good news about the rescue operation which God has effected in Jesus Christ. It is the message that our yearning for eternal life, which started growing perhaps independently of the church and then was nurtured and deepened and directed by the church, is to be satisfied. And indeed, in a sense, it is already satisfied, in that for the sake of Jesus, the perfectly humble one who loved with a pure spiritual love, God has counted us (the spiritual cannibals) fit for this kingdom. We can hope for it because Jesus pleads our case before the Father and the Father listens to his Son, indeed is of one heart with his Son.

To the person who has gone through the spiritual development that I have described in the last three chapters, the gospel of Jesus will be as food to the hungry and water to the thirsty.

It will not sound like an alien story, unfit for consumption by Modern Man, as those writers of the 1960s thought it was (see Chapter 1). Instead it will sound like just what the physician ordered; it will be heard "objectively" for what it is in itself: the good news of God.

I argued in Chapter 2 that emotions are "construals" of things, in terms that impinge upon our concerns. The gospel offers us a way of construing ourselves, our neighbors, the creation, and God himself; it is a conceptual filter, a principle of interpretation, by which we "see the world" in a new light. Through the gospel, God intends to bear fruit in people's hearts: the fruit of joy, peace, hope, thanksgiving, love, and more. But since these fruits of the message are emotions, they cannot be expected to arise if the hearer is not actively concerned about the things to which the message "speaks." The gospel "speaks" to the issues of sin and death, and says that the kingdom of God has been and will be established; and thus it "speaks" only to people whose hearts are more or less deeply exercised about these matters. In the last three chapters I have attempted to sketch the passion which would make emotional sense of the gospel of Jesus Christ: a yearning for an eternal life of moral purity. To people (even regular churchgoers) who are concerned only about their health, pleasures, reputation, real estate, and bank account, the gospel will not be greeted with joy and gratitude. But to those who have opened themselves to the fact of their death and who have become deeply enough developed ethically to know what sin is and hate it, the message of the kingdom can indeed be the source of a new emotional life. In the next three chapters I shall examine three aspects of that new life, three "fruits of the Holy Spirit": gratitude, hope, and compassion.

✳ 6 ✳
Gratitude

THE three emotions (gratitude, hope, and compassion) to be studied in the following three chapters are of course only a selection of the Christian virtues. I have hoped, by this selection, to represent the range of Christian emotions while at the same time achieving concreteness by the specificity of my analyses. Someone may object that my selection cannot be a wise one, since I leave out joy and love, which figure so prominently in the pages of the New Testament. But "joy" is less the name of a Christian emotion than a name for a characteristic of many of the Christian emotions. Love, hope, peace, and gratitude are all joyful emotions, and I suspect that when one has said enough about these others, there will be nothing left to say about joy. "Love" is similarly a broad term, covering a number of emotion-related virtues such as patience, kindness, forbearance, humility, forgiveness, compassion, and generosity (see 1 Cor. 13:4-6). I have selected compassion to represent the love virtues. It is, like other members of its class, a virtue with obvious and immediate consequences for behavior toward other people. Gratitude, on the other hand, relates the believer directly to God, whereas hope relates him or her to God's future kingdom. But even in these three rather different emotions there are obvious interactions or overlappings. Gratitude to God for his compassion in Christ, while a form of loving fellowship with God, is also a motive for compassion toward one's needy neighbor. So compassion is an "expression" of gratitude. The kingdom hoped for in Christian hope is a large part of that for which the believer owes the debt of gratitude to God. And compassion is more than just the disposition to help people in need; it is seeing the needy neighbor in the light of God's mercy in Christ and the prospect of the kingdom.

W E must begin by distinguishing gratitude from gratitude loosely so-called. "We were so grateful to get a home mortgage at only 12½ percent interest," I hear someone say. And I ask, "grateful to whom?" Not to the mortgage company, for 12½ percent was just the going rate that day. Not to the pace-setting banks in New York, who raised the prime rate two days after our loan was approved (they certainly didn't wait for *us*). To God, then, who in his provident wisdom timed things so that we got in at 12½ percent, whereas the folks whose loans were approved two days later had to pay 13½ percent? No, for it turns out that the "grateful" couple in question does not believe in God. I call this "gratitude loosely so-called" because there is no answer to the question, "grateful to whom?" Instead of saying "we were so grateful . . ." they might as well have said, "we were so glad. . . ." There is no person, even vaguely conceived, to whom thanks are conceived to be due for the happy way the circumstances fell out.

Gratitude has in view that *for which* thanks are due, and that person or persons *to whom* thanks are due. You can't be grateful for nothing, and you can't be grateful to no one; for in either case, you are not grateful — though you may be very cheerful, glad, ecstatic, exultant, and even flushed. Furthermore, you can't be unconcerned about either that for which thanks are due or the person to whom thanks are due and still be grateful. At the moment that I am writing these words my wife Elizabeth is seeing to it that I have the peace and quiet necessary to finish this book by protecting me against unnecessary intrusions. I am grateful to her for this peace and quiet because I want to finish the book and because I am glad to be dependent on her for such goods as this. If she showered me with a matching set of hungry, energetic, and otherwise salivating Labrador retriever puppies, I would be glad of her love even though expressed in this awkward way, but I would not be grateful for the gift. On the other hand, if a wealthy relative who all her life has sought to remake me in her own patrician image leaves me a large sum of money, I may be glad for the gift, but not grateful to the donor. For I may perceive the gift as one last posthumous effort in a thirty-year series of efforts to deliver me against my will from the company of beloved philistines. Gratitude always implies a happy perception of the relationship between the beneficiary and the benefactor. I can be grateful to Elizabeth for guarding my peace and quiet because I am glad to be dependent on her for important things. But since I am not glad to be dependent on my overbearing relative, I am also not able to be grateful to her.

Thus gratitude, like other emotions, is a construal (or set of interlocking construals) determined by concerns. In gratitude to my wife I construe her as my benefactor (i.e., the intentional giver of peace and quiet). Or alternatively, I construe my peace and quiet as a beneficence of my wife; or again, I construe myself as the beneficiary of my wife's grace. Whether my attention is chiefly directed at myself, my wife, or the benefit, does not matter; for in making any one of these terms the object of the construal, the other two provide necessary background for the construal. Furthermore I *care* about both the gift and my relationship to the giver in determinate ways: I find the gift desirable and am glad to stand in the relation of dependency to the giver. Thus the concern for peace and quiet, in combination with the concern (or at least the willingness) to receive graces from my wife, constitute what I called in Chapter 2 an emotional disposition—in this case the disposition to be grateful to my wife for this gift. When I then construe her as having given me this gift, I have the emotion of gratitude.

But emotions are themselves dispositions—dispositions to behave in certain ways. Gratitude is a disposition to behave in "loving" ways—to kiss and hug and help, to praise and thank, to cooperate, be patient, forbear faults, not to insist on one's own way. There are three ways to interpret this fact, only one of which is true to gratitude.

First, you can think of the responsive behavior as a way of insuring that the benefactor continues to give. Thus if I hug and kiss Elizabeth as a way of making sure she continues to protect my peace and quiet, this is not an expression of gratitude, though she may think it is. I am not trying to say "thank you," but trying to get something out of her. I appreciate her willingness to help me not as something in itself precious, but only as a means to getting a job done—that is, protecting my peace and quiet.

A subtler distortion of gratitude conceives the responsive behavior as repayment. Out of a falsely applied sense of justice I may feel that I must repay my wife for her beneficence to me, so as to be free from the debt she puts me in by her grace. I must be patient, kind, forbearing, and so forth to even up the account and thus to assert my essential independence of her. Here I am not concerned, as above, to insure that she continues to give; I am concerned that the score be even. I am too "proud" to see myself as genuinely in her debt. But to make expressions of gratitude out to be an element in a commercial transaction means that they have ceased to be expressions of gratitude. In genuine gratitude I am glad to let the gift remain a gift—and as the recipient to remain eternally a debtor.

In true gratitude, the response to grace is seen neither as a way of manipulating the giver nor as a way of evening up the score, but as an act of love. Here the thankful individual is glad to be indebted to the benefactor because the debt binds him to the other. He rejoices in his own love behavior in the same way he rejoices in that of his benefactor—as a bond which binds the two together in fellowship. The important thing is the fellowship, the love itself—or to put the same thing another way, the important thing is the partner in the love relationship. There is no thought of keeping the score even—"justice" in this sense has been submerged in love—and even less is there any thought of using the love partner as a means of getting something.

So we see how important a person's concerns are to this matter of gratitude. Only a person cultivated in the concern for fellowship can be grateful.

CHRISTIAN gratitude differs from the ordinary gratitude I've been discussing not in its "logic," but in its "content." That is, in having *some* "to whom" and "what for" and in being grounded in *some* concerns, it does not differ at all from ordinary gratitude. It differs, rather, in whom specifically the gratitude is directed to, in what specifically the grateful person is thankful for, and in the particular concerns which ground the gratitude.

When St. Paul exhorts the Thessalonians to give thanks in all circumstances (1 Thess. 5:18), it is obvious that he means them to give thanks to God. It is less obvious what, in general, a Christian will give thanks *for*.

One answer to this question is offered in the popular series of "praise" books by Merlin Carothers. (My copy of *Power in Praise* claims on the cover that over six million "praise" books have been sold.) Carothers's thesis is that we are to thank God for everything that happens, no matter how evil it may seem to us. In his first three stories miracles are worked when a family begins to thank God that their father is an alcoholic, when a couple learns to thank God that their daughter is insane, and when a mother thanks God that her daughter has become a go-go dancer. This does not amount to an endorsement of alcoholism, insanity, and go-go dancing. In each case the evil is eliminated, and the miracle is attributed to the power of praise or to the power of God which is released when we praise him for all things. So, paradoxically, thanking God for Dad's alcoholism leads to the disappearance of it. And Carothers finds this entirely appropriate. (This suggests a certain asymmetry between thanking God for Dad's alcoholism and, say, thanking him that our child was born healthy. Even Carothers would think something amiss if we started noticing a correlation between our thanking God for our children's health and their ceasing to be healthy.) So thanking God for something does not seem to imply, for Carothers, that what we thank him for is not evil. But it does imply that God is the author of what we thank him for:

> The very fact that we praise *God* and not some unknown fate also means that we are accepting the fact that God is responsible for what is happening. Otherwise it would make little sense thanking *Him* for it. (*Power in Praise,* p. 2)

This consequence, which seems unavoidable if we praise God for everything that happens, is theologically unhappy. For if God is the author of everything that happens, he is the author of sin. Carothers fails to distinguish God's being in ultimate control of all things from God's being the author of all things. It can be true that God will see to it that all things work together for ultimate good without its being true that he wills and authors every individual thing that happens. Also it is not true, as Carothers claims, that there is biblical warrant for his practice. He appeals to 1 Thessalonians 5:16–18; but thanking God *in* all circumstances is not the same thanking God *for* all circumstances. He appeals to Romans 8:28, "We know that in everything God works for good with those who love him." But again, it is wrong to infer that since God works for good *in* circumstances of sin, the sins themselves have God as their source, and he must be thanked for them. In one verse Paul does, on an utterly literal reading of his words, exhort his readers to thank God for everything:

> And do not get drunk with wine, for that is debauchery; but be filled with the Spirit, addressing one another in psalms and hymns and spiritual songs, singing and making melody to the Lord with all your heart, always and for everything giving thanks in the name of the Lord Jesus Christ to God the Father (Eph. 5:18–20).

But when Paul says "for everything" here, shall we take him literally? Since he is not writing a treatise for theologians, but instead a letter in which he can assume that people will supply a missing qualifier here and there, it is reasonable that when he says "for everything" he might mean "for everything worthy." And I think this hypothesis will recommend itself to us if we try to imagine Paul giving thanks for the activities of the Judaizers in Galatia or the heretics in Corinth. I conclude that the practice of thanking God for everything is bad theology and lacks biblical warrant.

But still, Carothers has his finger on an important feature of the Christian faith, even if he has distorted it. In Christianity the "values" which govern ordinary human evaluation (and thus thanksgiving) have been revised. The "natural man" in us tends to think that esteem in the eyes of others, physical health, freedom of movement, wealth, accomplishments, position, power, superiority over others, and cleverness are the things that make life worthwhile. But Christianity has deep doubts, of different kinds, about these "natural values."

Some of them it sees as nonvalues and as temptations. For example, superiority over others may be a natural fact and a social necessity, but it is the sort of thing in which a Christian glories to his eternal peril (see Chapter 5). The love of power over others, a frankly approved passion among the heathen, is something the Christian will try to wipe from his heart. So if I have been struggling half-heartedly against this desire, and then something happens which frustrates it (maybe I don't get the promotion I've been longing for), I may thank God for this frustration. The natural man in me writhes, but the Christian in me sees the frustration as a blessing, as a device by which I am encouraged to die to myself and live to God and neighbor. Thanking God for such a frustration may look crazy to a heathen, but it's perfectly natural to a Christian, who views worldly success with a suspicious eye.

Other items in the list of worldly values the Christian will view not as nonvalues but as tricky *relative* values. Cleverness, health, and freedom of movement, for example, are good things for which God is to be thanked when he blesses us with them. But they are not the highest value, as the heathen may well think; for in the Christian scheme they are all to be overridden by the claim of God's kingdom. If a Christian is faced with a choice between his physical well-being and his relationship with God, he must choose the latter. But as we grow in the Christian life, we become aware how strongly inclined we still are to make these values of the "natural man" into the highest values. We talk big about God, but all our behavior and thoughts add up to a pretty convincing case that we live for money, reputation, and physical survival. It is to people like us that the words "You cannot serve God and mammon (or power, or health, or freedom)" are addressed. It is not the Christian's thinking mammon a good thing that is so bad, for it *is* a good thing. It is his *serving* it that makes it an evil for him. So he needs to be broken loose from it, wrenched away, detached, "liberated" from this false master. And the untoward events of our lives—the times in which we fail to make the money we want or to accomplish what we would like, or times in which our health or freedom is taken away from us—are ideally suited to become reminders to us that our true life is hid with God in Christ, and not to be found among these things. We can give thanks to God for such sufferings, as appointed instruments by which we are led back to him.

So when we thank God for the good days, we thank him differently than for the bad ones. For the good ones we thank him as for something good in itself, but for the bad ones as a discipline which purifies our love for him. Our inclination as "natural men" is to thank God only for the good days. But this means that we fail to understand two things: first, that we are eternal beings, made not for passing conditions such as wealth and fame and health of body, but for a relationship with God; and second, that we are at odds with God because we place ultimate value on these things and turn our backs on him. The danger is that when we thank God for good days, we will fall into the pattern of "serving" health and wealth and success and making God a mere means or provider of these things. The grateful person welcomes his dependency on his benefactor. Only one who desires *fellowship with God* can be grateful to him for the gifts he bestows. And, since no one can serve both God and a second master, only one who desires fellowship with God *above all else* desires fellowship with *God,* rather than some phantom God-substitute. By these standards none of us is perfected in gratitude to God. But we can grow in it, can make progress along the way to this happy fellowship with our eternal Father, by making sure that we thank him not only for things that seem immediately good to us but also for some that contravene our endlessly threatening project to make this present passing world our home.

This is surely the important truth that lies behind Carothers' practice of thanking God for everything. But because of the presence of sin in the world, the Christian cannot be as indiscriminate in his thanksgiving as Carothers recommends. He must exercise discernment, which in some cases may be difficult and risky, in deciding which untoward events to thank God for and which to ascribe to human sinfulness or other evil powers. It seems perfectly clear that in most cases I can thank God for the loss of my job or a failure to get a promotion. But can I thank God for the perverted upbringing that has brought a loved one of mine to a continual state of withdrawal from human company? This state of affairs seems to be the moral destruction of a person, directly traceable to human perversity. Am I then to thank *God* for it? I might justify thanking God for it on the grounds that the destruction of my loved one, like the loss of my promotion, can occasion my being thrown back in dependence upon God. But there is something perverse about seeing the degradation of a human being as a good because I (or anybody) learn a lesson from it. I can, of course, thank God for the lesson, a good that he has brought out of this terrible evil. But that is a long way from thanking him for the evil itself.

Why do many people find Carothers's practice so attractive and helpful? Because it is a powerful way of getting some mastery of our troubles. In the face of so much suffering, we feel ourselves victims of senselessness. Implicating God by the act of thanksgiving is a way of getting a visceral conviction that the suffering does not render life utterly senseless. Giving thanks for suffering resigns us to our situation. It is much more effective than just gritting our teeth and trying, by an act of pure will, to accept our situation. Often our lives are further complicated and our sufferings compounded by our refusal to accept what is unavoidable about our lives. We make ourselves both miserable and impotent by our sulking and resentment. So, as any Stoic could tell us, becoming willing to accept these things can be a large first step to restoring happiness and strength.

For people who are not used to thinking things through, even Carothers's theological and exegetical crudities are an attraction. One just bypasses the agonies of discernment and gets immediately down to the business of giving thanks. However, a theologically more adequate view, while lacking the virtue of simplicity, does preserve the other virtues of Carothers's practice. For if I thank God not for, say, the death of my loved one (the Bible does not give much warrant for thinking death a good thing), but for his presence with both me and my loved one *despite* his death, I cease to be an ultimate victim of an ultimate senselessness. I may not be able to make detailed intellectual sense of death, yet going to God in thanksgiving for the mercy in which I trust that death will not have the last word is a resource of equilibrium. And since in going to God in gratitude for those aspects of the situation for which I *can* give thanks, I affirm that God is ultimately in control, I also find myself able to accept the unchangeable aspects that I am so inclined to resist.

But a Christian does not have to look far or strain her mind in risky discernment to find reasons for gratitude. Surely what Paul had in mind when he exhorted the Thessalonians to give thanks in all circumstances was that they should be always ready to give thanks to God for his unspeakable gift of salvation in Jesus Christ. Jesus' reconciling death for sinners and his resurrection from the dead are circumstances which stand until the end of the world, transcending in human significance every other circumstance which may obtain, however fraught with sin, suffering, and death it may be. In faith we see ourselves surrounded by it on all sides: sin and death have been overcome, and we are destined for purity and an eternal kingdom; God has done this wonderful thing for us "while we were yet sinners," that our history as sinners might be swallowed up and transformed into another order of life. And so as we stand in any circumstances—of disappointment, moral defeat, or death—we can give thanks to our heavenly Father for what he has done for us in Jesus. And in that act of grateful fellowship we rise above our immediate circumstances and see them in the light of the absolute circumstance of God's love.

WE must turn now to the question of how we *become* grateful persons—Christians in the very heart, full of gratitude to God our creator and savior. How do we, whose hearts are habitually so dull, become the spontaneously grateful children that we were created to be? That is, how do we become spiritual in this very central attitude of thanksgiving?

We must take our clues from the fact that an emotion is a construal based on a concern and also from some of the specific points we have made about gratitude. According to our account, gratitude is a way of paying attention to any one (and thus all) of three things: oneself, God's gift, and God. It is a construal of any one of these things in the terms of the other two. It is "seeing" God as the giver of salvation, life, discipline, or some special good to myself. It is "seeing" myself as the one whom God has blessed with such a gift. Or, it is "seeing" my deliverance from sin and death, or my very existence, or some instance of discipline (some suffering) as God's gift to me. But a *mere* construal of my own existence as a gift from God would not be gratitude. For a construal may lack "seriousness" in two ways.

First, the construal may not have the seriousness of a belief, being instead merely an "entertaining the idea of" something in some terms. I can, by turns, construe my existence as a gift of God, as a curse from God, as a cosmic accident, or as a purely natural coincidence of material particles. As a Christian I believe that my existence is not a curse, a cosmic accident, or a purely natural coincidence; but my belief does not keep me from *entertaining* these other construals. Indeed, by momentarily construing the world as a secular humanist does, new light may be cast upon the beauties of the Christian life. He, by the same power of imagination, can construe the world in Christian terms without thereby having the emotions that a Christian has when *he* looks at the world in that way. So not all construals are emotions. However, most serious construals (though not all) are based on beliefs.

Second, the construal may lack seriousness by failing to have the required relation to the concerns of the construer. If Hank the gardener does not care about the welfare of his tomato plants, he will not experience anxiety when the weatherwoman predicts hail, even though the prediction causes him to construe the plants as endangered. Similarly, I may fail to feel grateful to God for redeeming me even if I believe he has redeemed me and (in church, say, or reading a book of theology) construe him as having done so, if I lack one or both of the concerns which we have seen to be the ground of gratitude: a concern for the gift and a concern (or at least a willingness) to be in the "debt" of the giver. Consequently, if I am to learn heartfelt thanks in all circumstances for his gift of redeeming me in Jesus Christ, I must develop a concern for redemption and a disposition to be glad to be dependent on God for it.

So far, then, our analysis has revealed three points at which Christian gratitude may fail to come to fruition: the construal may not have the seriousness of a belief; the individual may not care sufficiently about the gift that God bestows; and the individual may be unwilling to stand in the relationship of utter dependency on God that gratitude implies. Each of these points offers clues as to how persons can be nurtured in gratitude. Let us examine each one in turn.

It seems pretty obvious that the best way for a construal to gain the seriousness of a belief is for it to be grounded in a belief. So if it is a question of construing God as the bestower of redemption in Jesus Christ, the best way of lending seriousness to this construal is for people to *believe* that God has indeed redeemed them in Jesus Christ. Modern theology has made repeated efforts to skirt the "plain old believing" that I am talking about here. It is certainly true, as such theologians never tire of reminding us, that *pistis* in the New Testament is a richer and more deeply personal concept than this plain old believing. And it is possible that the older theologians, especially the hyperorthodox, were guilty of laying too much stress on "assent." The present analysis of Christian spirituality lays by far the greater emphasis on the nurture of appropriate concerns and patterns of "willing." But its claim that emotions are serious construals also commits us to plain old believing. I, at least, cannot see how we can hope to maintain the concrete Christian emotions, which are the very core of Christian spirituality, unless we assent to the beliefs that make our construals serious to us.

What then can be done when people's plain old believing in the Christian message falters? This question is misleading, because it suggests there is some one thing that might cure people of disbelief. But the grounds and causes of disbelief are so various that the most one can do is to "take 'em as they come." There are doubts which arise from misreadings of scripture, doubts based on false or doubtful historical hypotheses concerning Jesus or the origin of the texts concerning him, doubts grounded in fallacious reasoning, doubts based on epistemological confusions ("if God exists his existence ought to be provable to all comers"), doubts arising from a misunderstanding of the boundaries between ethical and scientific thinking and Christian thinking, and doubts caused by a lack of appreciation of the greatness of Christianity, to name just a few. Each of these grounds of doubt calls for a different strategy, and a discussion of these strategies belongs in a different book than the present one. (C. S. Lewis is usually very good on this kind of issue, and I have addressed some of these doubts in my book *Rudolf Bultmann's Theology*.)

So an inability to assent to the Christian message is one obvious way that Christian gratitude may be kept from coming to fruition. The second way is that a person may not care sufficiently about the gift that God has bestowed. For it often happens that even if we have no burning doubts about the Christian message, still our hearts are cold and we do not experience delighted loving fellowship with God. How are we to come to treasure the gift that he has bestowed on us in Jesus if we find our hearts thus cold? I would like to suggest that the answer to this question is to be found in the "passion" which I sketched in Chapters 3 through 5. There I argued that the concerns upon which emotions like Christian gratitude are based are generically human ones which, however, have been deepened and shaped in interaction with Christianity. They are the concern with what Christianity calls "sin and death."

I argued that as beings with a surveying imagination, we all have an intense concern with death, even though it may be covered up by the distractions of busyness. This deep concern, to which the gospel speaks, is there planted in the breast of every man and woman, in virtue of their nature. "Planted" is a good metaphor, because our concern with death is a seed of eternity in us which can grow into spirituality, even though we usually resist letting it do so. It is buried a fraction of an inch below the surface of consciousness most of the time, and we have many devices for getting it to stay there. We are afraid of being destroyed if we let it grow up into the light, where the light will cause it to grow even more. What if we're absurd, and the universe is just unsuited to the yearning we find in our deepest breast? Or, what if we actually came in touch with the eternal and had to turn our backs on the comforts and loves of this finite life? So if that ultimate question begins to peek up above the surface, we quickly shovel a bit more dirt on it. But distractions never quite succeed in delivering us from this disturbing seed. All the devices we employ to still the yearning only shove it a little below the surface, from which it menacingly pushes up again from time to time.

Since the Christian emotions are grounded on a clarified form of this concern for eternal life, it is essential to their development that the individual become transparent to himself, open to this need for eternity. He must not repress and divert it in fruitless ways, but struggle to own up to it, to dwell upon it and culture himself on it. Is it any wonder that persons whose lives have been trivialized by immersion in money, fame, competition, and sensuality find, when they hear the gospel, that they have difficulty feeling any gratitude to God—even if they are the churchy sort of people who are glad enough to assent to the message?

But the passion for eternal life which comes out when we honestly face our death is only the most primitive form of the passion upon which gratitude is founded. In interaction with Christianity (and to some extent with everyday ethics) this passion is shaped into an *ethical* one, a desire for "righteousness." It becomes clear that one does not enter into eternity, the presence of God, in just any sort of ethical condition of soul. God does not tolerate self-deceivers, sensualists, egotists, liars, cheats, neighbor-haters, scorners of the lowly, and ignorers of the poor and suffering. To stand in his presence, to be a member of his kingdom, one must be *fit* for it, and fitness in this case bears the name of righteousness.

So the desire to live eternally becomes the desire to be fit for the kingdom. But as the individual grows spiritually, he sees fitness less and less as a ticket—as just a way of getting what he really wants, which is eternal life—and sees it more and more as an essential condition. God is holy, and eternal life *is* acceptability before this holy God. The believer comes more and more to see God not as a little child sees her Daddy (as somebody who needs to be got around in order to get what she wants), but as an older child (who appreciates her father's viewpoint) sees her father. The very tendency to separate the desire for eternal life from the desire for purity of heart comes to be morally abhorrent.

So the passion for eternity has been transformed into an ethical passion, the passion to be *fit* for eternity. This is another crucial element in "passional education in gratitude." Not only is it necessary that the disciple become transparent (which, by the way, is already a partially ethical task) but he must also take a passionate, striving interest in becoming fit for the kingdom of God—in comporting himself, in thought and deed, in such a way as to express that God, the source of the moral law, is *king*. But the passion to be fit for eternity always, in this life, ends up in a frustrating split within the person: the split between the desire for righteousness and the willingness to live in unrighteousness. At the height of self-awareness this split is intolerable and the individual has the tendency to back off from the requirement and mendaciously settle for something less. The good news is that while God cannot tolerate anyone in his kingdom who isn't fit for it, nevertheless we have been welcomed into it because of Jesus our representative. He, the one who *is* fit for it, has become the representative of us the unfit, so that we might be considered fit by the only one whose consideration makes any difference. Under the mercy of this good news it becomes possible to live with the frustration which attends hungering and thirsting for righteousness while being in bondage to sin. The gospel keeps the passion for righteousness alive, keeping us from despair over our recalcitrant sinfulness.

Thus the developing passion in us can become, in response to this gospel, the basis of gratitude. The gift of salvation which God offers is precisely what we want. We live this life by constantly striving toward and failing to live up to an ideal. But that ideal is constantly fulfilled apart from our striving because of the atonement in Jesus Christ. God speaks to our hearts because our hearts are filled with the desire for him that he has satisfied in Christ.

So the answer to the question, What can we do about it if we do not care sufficiently about the gift that God has bestowed? is obvious. We must practice self-transparency so that our yearning for eternity can become explicit and strong. And we must undertake the ethical task of becoming fit for the kingdom of God—even though we know, as Christians, that we will not succeed in this life, nor even in the next apart from the help he offers us in loving and accepting us just as we are. It seems to me that Christian counselors, spiritual directors, teachers, preachers, and writers could do much to foster the passion which is at the basis of the Christian emotions, and thus to foster the Christian emotions themselves, by constantly holding up to ourselves and to others the task of becoming transparent and the task of becoming heartfit for the kingdom. The most appropriate and powerful way of doing this is probably indirect—by becoming transparent moral strivers ourselves, and letting this trait become a subtle, pervasive trait of our teaching and writing. The superficiality of much Christian teaching these days, and its consequent ineffectiveness in nurturing people, is due to its lacking this "passionate" character.

THE third condition of gratitude which our analysis revealed was this: a person cannot be grateful for a gift if she is not willing or eager to be in a relation of loving dependence upon the giver. In the last section, in expounding the consequences of the second condition, I focused on the most basic kind of Christian gratitude: gratitude for salvation. In relation to this kind of gratitude, it is not possible to fulfill the second condition — an enthusiasm for the gift — without fulfilling also the third — a willingness to be dependent on the giver. For if someone has come to treasure salvation, she has come to cherish the relation of loving dependency on God. Of course she may have a perverted notion of salvation. If she thinks of it as just living forever or as civic righteousness, then she may want salvation without wanting to be dependent on God for it. But such a conception of salvation is not Christian.

So it will be useful now to turn our attention to the other, less central, objects of thanksgiving for a moment. If we find ourselves glad enough for some of God's gifts, such as our life, our health, and the means for sustaining these, but we are not glad to accept them from *him,* what can we do about it? We cherish health and life, but want to be autonomous, self-sufficient, "men come of age." It is not only self-avowedly secular people or self-declared Pelagians who have this hang-up about thanksgiving, but also we churchier and more orthodox types much of the time. We like God's gifts all right (just as I like the inheritance from my overbearing aunt), but we are less than enthusiastic about receiving them from *him.*

The diagnosis of this deficiency in our gratitude, and the strategy for curing it, are obvious. One who is glad to receive gifts from God but who is not grateful to God for them is one who lacks a passion for eternity; through a lack of transparency and moral striving shaped by the gospel of God, she feels fulfilled by her present human relationships, her possessions, her work, and other finite connections. Or, if she feels unfulfilled, she thinks of herself as basically satisfiable by some *changes* in these finite connections. She has not learned to desire the kingdom which includes this perfect fellowship of dependency. The cure for this form of ingratitude is, then, the same as for ingratitude based on a failure to appreciate God's ultimate gift: that the individual enter, with the help of members of the Christian community, upon the task of becoming transparent to herself and of learning to hunger and thirst for righteousness.

We have taken our clues about education in Christian gratitude from the fact that gratitude is a serious construal of God as the giver of gifts to us. We must not overlook the simple but important fact that gratitude is a construal *at all.* An emotion is a way of *paying attention* to something, of *dwelling on the thought* of something. We can bring ourselves to dwell on the thought of something in many ways: by talking about it, by thinking about it, by reading about it, by performing some action with respect to it, or even just by turning our attention toward it. Part of the reason that we worship God regularly is to exercise ourselves in construing him as our Lord, ourselves as his people, and our fellow Christians as our brothers and sisters in Christ. If gratitude requires that we construe God as the giver of gifts to us, it stands to reason that a crucial way of becoming a grateful person is to get in the *habit* of thinking of God in this way. Praising God in words, in songs, in silent thoughts, and in actions which are expressions of gratitude are the primary ways of exercising ourselves in gratitude. As we do so again and again over the years, seeing our lives and sustenance as God's gifts to us, seeing ourselves as the objects of his mercy in Jesus Christ, and seeing our sufferings as disciplines by which he draws us closer to himself, the emotion of gratitude becomes second nature to us, a trait of our deepest personality.

❈ 7 ❈
Hope

HOPE is a happy construal of our future, or of some aspect of it. Like other emotions, hope is not possible unless an appropriate concern is in place; the object of hope is always something the individual *wants,* whether it be a trivial hope like sunshine for tomorrow's picnic, an important but finite one like the recovery of a loved one from an illness, or the ultimate one of sharing the glory of God.

So hope differs fundamentally from another rather benign attitude to the future, resignation. If I am resigned to the future, then though I don't welcome it, I have succeeded in tolerating its prospect. It doesn't make me happy, but at least it doesn't cast me very deeply into despair or dread. Resignation too is based on a concern. It makes no sense to resign myself to an aspect of the future about which I am unconcerned. But in resignation I purposely dull my concern, refusing to let it be as active as it would otherwise tend to be. I protect myself against the unhappiness of the prospect by curbing either my enthusiasm for what my future denies me or my repugnance for what the future holds.

Resignation, then, is a way of tolerating the future, but hope is a way of welcoming it. Resignation means that we live life by dulling certain concerns, some of which are fundamental to our nature as persons: for example, the concern for life and the concern for a humanly worthy life. (A person who has resigned *these* concerns is a kind of spiritual suicide.) Hope allows these fundamental passions to grow and flower and dig their roots deep. Resignation is a way of coping with life, of making shift when hope seems impossible. But he who hopes does not merely get by; he lives with the gusto and openness of a full human life.

The apostle says, "May the God of hope fill you with all joy and peace in believing" (Rom. 15). But what if Paul had been a secular humanist? If he was also transparent to himself about his situation in the universe, he might have said "May the God of resignation fill you with tolerance for your destiny," or "May the benign Void enable you to quell your yearnings for eternity," or "May the God of cosmic process make you magnanimous enough to accept your absorption into his consequential nature"—but he would not have talked about joy and peace. Of course, the resigned secular humanist may have a *kind* of peace; if he is really resigned to his obliteration and also to the destruction of all the highest ideals of moral perfection, he may possibly be tranquil about his destiny. If he catches himself, now and then, yearning for something beyond death and something above the moral sordidness of his present heart and his present social existence, he may quiet his yearning enough to keep him from despair. It is a matter of judgment whether we should call this "peace." But even if we honor it with this name, we must note that it will not be a *joyful* peace, like that of the hopeful person. He will be at peace in the sense that he is no longer, like the unresigned unbeliever, desperately longing for a different destiny than the one he expects. However, he will not be at peace in the sense that he *welcomes* his future.

But as our earlier discussions have suggested, the usual substitute for hope (even among us churchgoers) is not a courageous and lucid resignation in the face of oblivion and unrighteousness, but a cowardly self-darkening about ourselves and a dulling of concern about the deeper reaches of mortality. To the unnerving deliverances of our surveying imagination we respond by burying our hearts in finite hopes. We send our eternal selves out prospecting on earth, where moth and rust and time consume and bad fortune breaks in and steals our hopes away. And as long as reality does not crash in to destroy the houses of cards in which we dwell, we find here just enough satisfaction of our need for hope to keep us from despair—and also from faith.

Somewhere short of the totally secularized Christianity I have just described is the attempt we so often note in ourselves of a compromise between Christianity and secularism: "I shall give myself without reservation to the projects and prospects of this earthly life, but just in case something goes wrong, I'll make my peace with Jesus. Religion is, after all, supposed to be a comfort in times of trouble, and let's be realistic: troubles don't *always* happen to the other guy. I may croak before my projects are all complete, and it would be a pity if I had nothing to fall back on." This attitude leaves something to be desired as a passion for the kingdom of God. For Christians the kingdom hoped for is the focusing goal of life, to which everything else is made subsidiary. But in the attitude I have just described the kingdom is not the pearl of great price, the crown of life, the one thing needful. Instead, it is a sort of consolation prize for those who don't do very well in the race. Just as no man can serve two masters (if God is one of the masters), so no man can have two hopes (if the kingdom is one of the hopes). This man does not have the joy and peace of Christian hope; instead, he combines a comically mild form of resignation with a false conception of the kingdom.

The developed Christian lives in hope—in happy anticipation of participating in God's eternal kingdom where the rule of heart and action is perfect love. Hope differs both from the resignation of the lucid secularist and from the burial in earthly projects of John Q. Doe and his cousins Average Presbyterian and Whoso Methodist. But hope nevertheless *presupposes* a kind of resignation and *enables* a hearty involvement in earthly projects and hopes.

WHAT devastates the eternal self is not that it has earthly hopes, but that it ascribes to them a status and significance they can't bear. Earthly hopes will not let a person down if she does not overinvest in them. But such is the passion of the human self that if it lacks a relationship with God it has a strong (if not irresistible) tendency to invest so much of itself in its earthly projects that their unreliability, their being subject to disappearance, and their fundamental unsatisfactoriness become the ground of despair. It becomes clear even to many who believe in nothing eternal—neither God nor his kingdom—that "salvation" is to be found in some kind of detachment from the objects of such hopes. Thus the attempt at peace which the lucid secularist makes through resignation.

But the resignation of the nonbeliever is made problematic by his having no satisfactory future to put in place of the obviously unsatisfactory future of the earth. He needs hope, with its joy, but has to settle for resignation, with its sullen tranquillity. This lack of happiness in resignation makes it difficult, if not impossible, for the resignation of these earthly hopes to be very successful. The individual resigns himself to his death, but still finds a secret (desperate) joy in the future of his children or in the thought that his reputation will live on after his death. So his peace is fragile. The Christian, on the other hand, has a hope which may be able to fill her with joy and thus to fill the gap which is left when she sees through earthly hopes. Let's not underestimate, however, the difficulty which the Christian too will have in detaching herself from earthly hopes. Even if she is very serious, she will find that unhealthy attachments to earthly prospects sully her happiness until the end of life, not to mention the difficulties that may beset her believing in her eternal hope. But assuming that she has the courage to believe with some steadiness, she who is resigning only her earthly hopes would seem to have a better prospect of success than he whose earthly hopes are the only ones he has.

So the Christian who would hope in God must draw back from her investments in earthly hopes — because these are bound to let her down, but even more because she finds that they are in competition with her hope of sharing the glory of God. She, like sinners generally, is *embedded* in this passing world, so deeply committed to it that its transitoriness is her despair. But as a Christian she knows that this despair is a rejection of her relationship with God. To become free from this despair she must invest the ultimate prospects of her life in God alone; and that means a serious alteration of her attachment to her earthly hopes.

So far we have seen two advantages which the Christian has over the lucid secularist. First, since she is in a position to have real hope transcending all her finite hopes, she is capable of an honest joy in life. Second, her hope gives her a better prospect of succeeding in detaching herself from her earthly hopes. But there is a third advantage. The Christian is able to be less wary of her earthly hopes than the lucid secularist. In gratitude she receives from the hand of the God of hope the happy prospects which come to her in this earthly life. This means that she can rejoice in these exactly as befits limited hopes. Of course she cares whether they are fulfilled, and may care very deeply; but if they are not fulfilled, her eternal hope gives her a healthy perspective on her disappointments, and sustains her in joy and peace. The Christian (of course I am speaking of the ideal) neither over- nor underestimates the earthly prospects. Not only does the hope of glory enable her honestly to resign all earthly prospects; it also empowers her to take these prospects up again and appreciate them for what they are. Resigned to their *ultimate* unsatisfactoriness, and protected against *despair* over them, she can rejoice and grieve, as is fitting, in the hopes and disappointments encompassed by her short earthly years. As she hopes, she is in a state of health with respect to earthly things. Unlike the Average Presbyterian, she sees them as they are; unlike the lucid secularist, the resignation by which she sees them as they are does not verge constantly on despair.

I want now to look at our subject from another angle and to think with you about the relations between hope as an emotion and two things that are closely tied to it, namely, the *mood* of hoping and hopefulness as a disposition or pervasive *attitude* — what we might call a character trait.

You have perhaps felt that my claim that emotions are construals is not true to emotions as we *feel* them. After all, are not emotions in some sense to be *contrasted* with thoughts? What about the old distinction between the mind and the heart, between the "cognitive" and the "emotive"? Have I not committed the philosopher's arrogant mistake of subsuming the heart under the mind, thus really denying the heart altogether? In making emotions ways of "seeing," have I not made them just a species of thought?

I admit to making emotions a species of thought, in some broad sense of that word, but not to denying the heart. As you will remember, emotions are not just *any* kind of construal; they are concern-based construals. But this answer may not quite satisfy you, for even concern-based construals are capable of being declared right or wrong by the kind of standards to which we subject judgments. If I judge that the people in the car behind me are following me with some sinister intent, I may be right or I may be wrong, and the basis on which I judge may be rational or irrational. But that judgment may also be the basis of the construal that generates anger or fear or indignation, and if so, then the emotion itself is either right or wrong, either rational or irrational. But, you will say, emotions are not either right or wrong, either rational or irrational; they are not the sort of thing that is subject to this kind of evaluation. Therefore, my view that emotions are construals must be wrong.

People who think that emotions are not subject to rational adjudication are usually confusing emotions with either sensations or moods. If you have a bodily sensation, such as an itch on your rump or a fluttery feeling in your diaphragm, it of course makes no sense to ask whether your itch or flutter are true or false, or based on good evidence or valid reasoning. An emotion cannot be a bodily sensation precisely because it can, like an opinion, be well- or ill-founded, and things like itches and flutters cannot. Hope, anger, envy, embarrassment, grief, and gratitude can obviously be rational or irrational, and if so, it follows that they can't be bodily sensations. Some emotions, especially those we share with the lower animals such as fear and anger, are associated with typical bodily sensations, such as dryness in the mouth, heat at the back of the neck, erection of the hair, an odd sensation in the abdominal or chest region, and trembling of the extremities. But these cannot be more than *accompaniments* of emotion, for the reason given above.

Emotions are also confused with moods. This is a more forgivable confusion, because of the close connection between emotions and moods. Moods, like sensations, are not subject to rational adjudication. Of course, they may be pleasant or unpleasant, and so may be good or bad, and a person may be irrational if he knowingly does something (like take some drug) which will put him in an unpleasant mood. But the mood itself cannot be correct or incorrect or based on good or bad reasoning. Moods are such states as being elated or cheerful, depressed or blue, and grumpy or irritable. If I ask, "Why do you have that itch?" you will answer not with a reason but a cause: "Because my wife washes my undies in hard water." Similarly if we ask, "Why is Daddy grumpy?" we are not asking for his reasons (reasonable or unreasonable), but for the causes of his state: "He hasn't had his dinner yet." Just as itches have various causes, so we are put in moods by various causes. Lack of sleep over a period of time can cause depression; caffeine causes irritability in some people and mild elation in others; deeply repressed factors in a person's psychiatric history inevitably have their influence on that person's moods and his susceptibility to them; different kinds of music seem to put people in tranquil, excited, or aggressive moods; cacophonous noises—one baby screaming, another banging on pots and pans, and someone else roaring away on a vacuum sweeper—make some people feel irritable; jogging long distances makes some people feel "high"; and of course narcotic drugs are notorious mood changers.

Another important cause of moods is emotions. If a person wins the lottery, she will very likely not only feel the emotions of joy and hope in seeing her financial situation changed for the better; very likely the cheerfulness of this emotion will "spill over" into other contexts. For a few hours, or days, or even weeks, she will have a "brighter outlook" on everything; her mind will be pervaded by a generalized optimism. Similarly, grief at the death of a loved one can "color" one's entire outlook on life for a period; the grief, which is clearly an emotion, begets a generalized depression, which is not an emotion but a mood. Thus we can see an important source of our temptation to think that moods are emotions. For sometimes when we ask, "Why is Daddy so grumpy?" we make indirect reference to an emotion and say, "Because he lost money on the farm sale." We do not mean that Daddy's reason for being grumpy is that he lost money on the farm sale. What we must mean is that Daddy's financial disappointment (an emotion) has *caused* him to sink into this grumpy state (a mood). His financial setback, by contrast, is a *reason* for his disappointment. Moods are not emotions, but since they are sometimes caused by emotions, we are inclined to think they are. And when we think of emotions as moods, it is natural to make the mistake of thinking that they are "irrational."

B UT the fact that moods are sometimes caused by emotions is not the only connection between the two. Moods also *predispose* emotions. I am, for example, more likely to dwell on the happy aspects of my future (and thus to experience hope) if I am in an even, optimistic, cheerful mood than if I am depressed. If I am in a severe depression I may not be able to "hear" the gospel at all; that is, I hear it with my ears all right, but do not succeed in construing my future in its terms. But being in an optimistic mood is not the same as hoping; hope is, as we have seen, a construal of the future in some terms, and Christian hope is the construal of our future in terms of God's promises of eternal life and righteousness.

It seems to me that one of the main purposes of the ornamental aspects of our worship services is to produce moods in the worshipers which are conducive to worshipful states of mind (joy, peace, contrition, hope, gratitude). The high-vaulted ceiling of the building may lead to a mood of exaltation, the colors and quiet of the sanctuary to a peaceful mood, the music—above all the music!—to a variety of moods: melancholia to go with contrition; cheer to go with joy, gratitude, love, and hope; triumph to go with hope. It seems that these features of the service are not just aesthetically "fitting," but actually tend to cause moods in us which are conducive to the Christian emotions. So these aesthetic or ornamental features of the service serve partially as aids to our having the Christian emotions in the midst of the worship service.

However, dangers attend this strategy. First, in highly "liturgical" services as well as some of the more colorful pentecostal services, the mood setting is so powerful that the worshipers may be inclined to mistake the moods they experience in church for Christian emotions. This is especially true where the worshipers are encouraged to seek religious "experiences." If the minister does a lot of *talking* about hope and joy in the Lord, and the importance of having these, and at the same time is engineering the service to produce moods of exaltation and triumph, it will not be surprising if the congregation tends to take these moods for Christian experience. But of course there is nothing peculiarly Christian about moods of exaltation and triumph, even if they are caused by Christian worship services; people led to mistake this mood for Christian emotions are being deceived. In the complacency begotten by rich, noncognitive Sunday experiences, they are partially immunized against real Christianity. I think that ministers often do this sort of thing to their congregations quite innocently; they are themselves as much victims of the confusion as their people. But once they learn to distinguish the Christian emotions from moods which a worship service can induce, it could become an important minor part of preaching and Christian education to clarify for their people this danger of "sentimentalizing" Christian faith.

But even if people do not confuse Christian emotions with the moods produced by the worship service, there is another danger connected with engineering the service for emotion. Let us say that an individual goes to church, hears the word of the gospel, and with gladsome mind construes his eternal future in terms of it. Thus he experiences Christian hope. But he also needs to be warned, directly or indirectly, that the educative purpose of the worship service is not that he should experience hope *in the service,* but that by the experience of hope that he has there, he should be on his way to becoming a hopeful *person.* The worship service is, after all, an artificial context, rather unlike the contexts in which he must live most of the hours and days of his life. The hope he experiences there should become a deeply etched hopefulness—a disposition so ingrained that it could be called a character trait—which he carries into the most diverse and unconducive situations of his life, situations where the environment, unlike the church, does not at all predispose him to hope, but where he must carry his hopefulness, environmentally unsupported, in his own heart. Hopefulness becomes a kind of toughness in him, an independence from his environment, a way in which he transcends his immediate situation.

John Calvin gives eloquent expression to the incongruity between the Christian's hope and the environment in which he lives:

> To us is given the promise of eternal life—but to us, the dead. A blessed resurrection is proclaimed to us—meantime we are surrounded by decay. We are called righteous—and yet sin lives in us. We hear of ineffable blessedness—but meantime we are here oppressed by infinite misery. We are promised abundance of all good things—yet we are rich only in hunger and thirst. What would become of us if we did not take our stand on hope, and if our heart did not hasten beyond this world through the midst of the darkness upon the path illumined by the word and Spirit of God! (Quoted in Jurgen Moltmann, *Theology of Hope,* pp. 18–19)

Thus even in the most intimate confrontation with sin and death, the Christian in whom hope has become a character trait can experience joy and deep equilibrium. In a letter which C. S.

Lewis wrote two months before he died, this joyful equilibrium comes out clearly:

> What a pleasant change to get a letter that does *not* say the conventional things! I was unexpectedly revived from a long coma, and perhaps the almost continuous prayers of my friends did it—but it [would] have been a luxuriously easy passage, and one almost regrets having the door shut in one's face. Ought one to honour Lazarus rather than Stephen as a protomartyr? To be brought back and have all one's dying to do again was rather hard.
>
> When you die, and if "prison visiting" is allowed, come down and look me up in Purgatory.
>
> It *is* all rather fun—solemn fun—isn't it? (Quoted in R. T. Herbert, *Paradox and Identity in Theology*, p. 174)

Being able to carry one's hope into situations which to the worldling would appear most contrary to hope; to experience the hope of life in the midst of death and the hope of righteousness amidst the unspeakable moral degradation of the present world—is it possible that this is what the apostle Paul has in mind when he connects Christian hope with "endurance" and "character" (Romans 5) and with "steadfastness" (Colossians 1, Romans 15)?

I turn now to the question of what we can do to nurture hopefulness in ourselves. How can one grow in integral hopefulness? How can one become, not just a liturgical hoper, but a "secularized" hoper, one in whom hope has become a toughness and a transcendence for all situations? Of course there is no way to guarantee against doubts, weakness of will, periods of "spiritual dryness," and even loss of faith. But there are surely disciplines that we can undertake to foster a resiliency of hope.

Why is our hope so weak? Why does the prospect of an eternal happiness seem so dim compared with the prospects of earthly happiness? Why does it occur to us, again and again in the Christian life, that this hope of glory is just a fiction, an empty dream?

We are perhaps inclined to think it's because the hope of sharing the glory of God is just intrinsically improbable. After all, nothing we can observe in nature would tend to support it;

indeed the whole "style" of nature seems to contradict it. Beside the achievements of knowledge in the natural sciences, this hope seems so utterly unsupported. Isn't it just a fantasy woven by the human mind? Isn't our life really something like that which Tolstoy describes somewhere: "In infinite time, in infinite space is formed a bubble-organism, and that bubble lasts a while and bursts; and that bubble is Me."

There are, of course, the hints: the resurrection of Jesus (without which it is very difficult to see how the Christian church got going); the testimony, which many deep people have found compelling, of the Holy Spirit; the congruency which the promise of the kingdom has with the deepest yearnings of some of the most intelligent human spirits. But there are alternative explanations of all these things; every one of them can be construed in purely naturalistic terms. So, in the last analysis, the hope of glory is just what the church has (almost) always said it is: a matter of venturesome *faith.* Objectively we are given, at most, ambiguous clues. The certainty of hope, if such certainty exists, must come from the kind of life we live, the kind of persons we are, the quality of our daily interaction with God and our fellow human beings. We must be people who trust in God and trust in those impulses which put us in touch with him; we must nurture not the naturalistic spirit in us, but the one that whispers to us (most of the time) that life is more than bubble-organisms in space-time.

In the first chapter of his letter to the Romans, the apostle Paul has this to say:

> Therefore, since we are justified by faith, we have peace with God through our Lord Jesus Christ. Through him we have obtained access to this grace in which we stand, and we rejoice in our hope of sharing the glory of God. More than that, we rejoice in our sufferings, knowing that suffering produces endurance, and endurance produces character, and character produces hope, and hope does not disappoint us, because God's love has been poured into our hearts through the Holy Spirit which has been given to us.

The New Testament writers speak rather frequently of rejoicing in sufferings, although their rationale for this varies. If the suffering is in the form of persecution on account of Christ, then the rationale for rejoicing is often that the suffering is a token of the disciple's bond with Christ, whose work on earth was so largely a matter of suffering (Acts 5, 1 Peter 4, Colossians 1). On the other hand, sufferings in general—not just persecutions, but calamities and the kind of suffering which leads Paul (Romans 8) to say that "creation was subjected to futility"—can have a spiritually instructive or upbuilding effect, which is a ground for rejoicing. This seems to be what is in view in 2 Corinthians 12 and Hebrews 12, as well as Romans 5. How do sufferings educate us in hope?

It is perhaps not quite true that hope springs *eternal* in the human breast, but even if we take this saying as a poetic exaggeration, it expresses a truth about human nature. There is a prereflective optimism built into us, one deeply confirmed given a happy childhood, which gives us resiliency in the midst of suffering and a tendency to hope in the face of dismal prospects. It is not built on any actual calculation of prospects or even the most cursory reckoning with actual possibilities. In this way it is a little bit like a mood. Yet it would not be quite right to call it a mood either, since "mood" seems to suggest a state that comes and goes and that differentiates individuals who have it from those who don't; but this optimism that springs almost eternal seems to exist as a feature of human nature, and it is dispelled (or deeply altered) only by very great trials.

This animal hopefulness is present, mixed with pessimism and more or less realistic assessments of the future, in all of us. But it is evident in its purer forms in children and adolescents, and very occasionally in a highly unreflective or sheltered adult. It is a disposition to look for the happy elements of the future, and not to dwell on the dark side; and so it is, like a mood, a predisposition to construe the future in happy terms. But insofar as this disposition finds its concrete hopes within the present mortal life, there is always a dissonance between the prereflective optimism and the concrete hopes in which it issues, a dissonance brought out by reflecting on the passing nature of this life. The dissonance is that the hopes in which the optimism becomes an emotion are always equally grounds for pessimism. The optimism which springs almost eternal is one which ill-fits earthly hopes, but nicely fits an eternal hope. One of the aims of Christian education is that this prereflective, moodlike animal hopefulness be transformed and fulfilled in the solid emotion of an eternal hope.

So the hope of sharing the glory of God is an enduring hope, tailored to our eternal nature, a hope that will not let us down. But *our* hoping in its terms is very far from solid and enduring. The object of our hope is eternal, but our hope itself is the very opposite, an up-and-down thing, shifting with our circumstances and our moods, with the company we keep and the books we happen to be reading. We sometimes feel it in church, but then, out in the world, it dissolves. Magnificent resolutions to have our hope in God alone are followed in a few minutes by the old patterns of trusting in our schemes and the probabilities of finite prospects, and doing our best to conceal from ourselves the blatant deception in which we are indulging.

T HIS is where our sufferings can come in, for Paul says that suffering produces endurance, and endurance character, and character a hope that does not disappoint us. Suffering can stabilize the hope of glory in us, giving it that toughness that makes it a secular, nonchurchy thing, that delivers it from dependence on organ music and oratory, on pastoral "presence" and weather and the last book read, and makes it a principle of our persons which we carry into unsupportive situations. What kind of sufferings can educate us in Christian hope? I think it is not so much the *kind* of suffering that is important, but what we *do* with it. Loneliness, betrayal by family or friends, the triumph of one's enemies, the impotence of disease or old age, the death of a loved one, a disappointment in business or love, hatred and opposition by other people—these all can help to teach us Christian hope, if only we take the right attitude toward them. How ought we to construe such sufferings?

A suffering can become a viscerally moving symbol of the present world's unfitness to satisfy my deepest needs. It can become a reminder, more vivid than any mere *word* of truth, that the present passing world is not my home—that I am a sojourner, a passer through. And so sufferings can become a powerful aid in getting the right perspective on the prospects which the world holds out. The Christian does not despise those prospects, as one might who did not believe that God created this present world; but he learns from his sufferings not to put his deepest heart into those prospects, and to reserve it instead for what is promised in the gospel.

I can meditate for weeks or months on the futility of life apart from God's kingdom. But if my own life is progressing gloriously and veritably glowing with earthly hopes — if there is nothing in it to make a strong *impression* on me of that futility — the meditation may not have the power to detach me significantly from my earthly prospects. While I may know that such prospects do not deserve an ultimate trust, this "knowledge" remains purely intellectual. But a suffering, rightly construed, can bring that knowledge into my heart, fostering the hope of glory as an enduring trait of my character. And when a Christian sees how his sufferings are training him in a hope that does not disappoint, he learns to rejoice in them.

But it takes vigilance to allow these sufferings to be teachers of hope. When a suffering comes upon me, my first inclination is not to take it as an ally in my struggle to detach myself from earthly hopes, but instead to see it in one of two ways. First, I may just see it as something to rid myself of as quickly as possible, so as to get back to my normal, happy, worldly state of mind. This is worldliness pure and simple. Of course the Christian too will welcome relief from her sufferings (they are, after all, sufferings), but she is willing to dwell in them for a while, draw them into herself, recognize them as a "normal" part of earthly existence and not something to be surprised or enraged about. She lets them sink in and become part of her world view; and afterwards, if they pass, she does not reject them as something totally alien to herself, but remembers thoughtfully that this too is the sort of thing that makes up earthly existence.

The second worldly way is to wallow in sufferings. This is perhaps not so obviously worldliness, since I do take a certain joy in the sufferings, and do not dissociate myself from them as in the first way. But it still is worldliness, since the sufferings do not become a means of relating myself happily to God and his kingdom. Wallowing admits of several forms, the chief among which are dragging others into the muck, turning the muck into a ground of superiority, and getting the universe into one's debt. Some people turn their suffering to a morbid sort of rejoicing by groaning and complaining and palling social gaieties with gloomy dicta. Thus they assure that others will feel miserable along with them. Their own sufferings become a convenient point of departure for the pleasures of sadism. Still others derive from their sufferings a sense of superiority over the happy people in the world, as though suffering per se somehow qualified them as more deeply human than the uninitiated. Still others get a sense of ascendancy by thinking roughly along these lines: "I have been wronged by the universe. It clearly owes me something for the suffering I am going through, and I can at least rejoice in that. And if unjustly (O cruel injustice of Being itself!) it does not pay off with happiness hereafter—well, that's fine too, because it is thus all the more indebted, indeed perhaps eternally indebted, to me."

The Christian, by contrast, does not rejoice in her sufferings out of sadism or any sense of superiority, but because they bring her into closer communion with God. However, there are two kinds of sufferings which we may doubt to be capable of this educational value. One is the sense of abandonment by God, and the other is intense physical pain.

People who are disposed to communion with God sometimes have periods in which God seems to be cruelly absent. The warmth of fellowship with him, the satisfactions of prayer, and the comfort and joy of faith have disappeared; the person experiences dull anxiety, depression, and a kind of guilty grief. This is not just the absence of faith—many people lack faith, yet experience no suffering over it—but it is the more intense feeling of abandonment. It seems a veritable contradiction that a person should take *this* suffering as a symbol of the necessity of hoping in God alone. Her suffering *is* her inability to hope in God, if we mean by "hope" to *feel* hopeful in him, to *construe* him as the ground of her ultimate prospects. Being not a worldly suffering, it cannot become a symbol of the inadequacy of the world; it is a spiritual suffering, and so if it is to be a symbol it must be a symbol of *ultimate* disappointment—even God cannot be trusted.

So this kind of suffering does not educate in the way that more ordinary sufferings can do; and yet it too can have an educational effect. One of the distortions into which the believer is likely to fall if she becomes too athletic in the spiritual use of worldly sufferings is to think herself too much the author and controller of her faith and hope. But faith and hope, like every good and perfect gift, come down from above, and to be perfect they must also be so understood. St. Paul says that "hope does not disappoint us, because God's love has been poured into our hearts through the Holy Spirit which has been given to us." And this "pouring" of God's love into the thirsty heart of the sufferer is a typical, if not very frequent, experience of Christians. A woman is praying in the darkness of abandonment, praying more out of a sense that she *ought* to be doing so than out of any sense of genuine encouragement. Perhaps she has been in this state for weeks or months. Though she continues her religious exercises, it has occurred to her more than once that she has become an unbeliever. And then suddenly out of the spiritual darkness, God's love floods in upon her, and her joy and hope are renewed more powerfully and deliciously than she could ever have thought possible. It is as though God is saying, "*I* am your hope and your salvation; in me alone you will trust, and not alone for your salvation but even for the faith by which you grasp it."

The other kind of suffering about which we may have doubts is intense physical pain. Otherwise faithful people, for whom "mental" sufferings are spiritually usable, find that physical sufferings obliterate their consciousness of God and their concern for anything other than the pain. I find this to be my own case, but am not convinced I ought to be complacent about this state of my soul. More spiritually mature people are able to turn physical pain to spiritual advantage. There is plenty of physical self-torture in the history of ascetical spirituality, though the attitude toward pain is not always healthy in that context. A healthy attitude is evinced by that remarkable English woman, Edith Barfoot of Oxford, who turned relentless physical suffering into a "vocation" of service to God and man which made her one of the most joyful Christians of our time. Her own account, along with the witness of a number of her friends, has been edited and published by Sir Basil Blackwell as *The Witness of Edith Barfoot.*

So far in this chapter we have found more grounds to be suspicious of worship services than we have to be hopeful about their effect on our spiritual development. The preoccupation with what happens *in* the service and the engineering of the service to "affect" people by the architecture, the music, the decoration of the sanctuary, and the voice, diction, and poetical powers of the preacher skew the emphasis away from character building and toward "experiences." I have tried to correct that emphasis a bit by talking, as the apostle Paul does, about the connection between suffering and the "steadfast" or "enduring" character of the Christian emotions. These emotions begin to count spiritually only when they become ingrained as character traits, only when the individual becomes steadfastly disposed to see the world in their terms. But we also have seen that hope, as conceived in Christianity as well as in ordinary life, is more than a mood and more than a prereflective optimism. It is instead a construal, a way of "seeing" the future. As such it is a way of focusing attention, of dwelling on the future—a way, we might even say, of experiencing the future. And as such it has to be something that happens at this or that specific moment of the day when our mind turns to our eternal future. Consequently it is fitting to have a regular context in which to dwell upon the mercies of God and turn our attention to the future he has prepared for us. So worship services, though they can be misleading, can be important to our spiritual development.

The idea of an *act* of gratitude is quite natural. Christians and non-Christians alike daily perform acts of gratitude whenever they say thank you to one another, write thank you notes, and return favors. Such acts can of course be perfunctory or insincere, but they may equally be occasions for the grateful focusing of attention on the giver, the gift, or oneself as beneficiary. Thus for the Christian, prayers of thanksgiving as well as acts of neighbor-love are not just "expressions" of thanksgiving to God but are also "exercises" of it, in both senses of the word: they are both the performance of construing things gratefully and the discipline of learning to do so with greater regularity, naturalness, and profundity.

The idea of an analogous act of hope seems less natural. There does not seem to be any act or family of acts in general human life which would qualify as acts of hope. But Christians have such an act in the service of the Eucharist. Rightly used, the Lord's Supper becomes at the same time an act of remembrance and an act of anticipation: remembrance of the suffering of Jesus through which we have been declared fit to enter into God's presence and start our long trek of sanctification in his fellowship; and anticipation of the perfection in which that process will one day issue. The Eucharist is a stated time for dwelling on the future which God has promised us in Christ. And so it is fully as much an "exercise" of hope as prayers of thanksgiving are an "exercise" of gratitude.

The Christian's life is punctuated and buoyed up by the acts of hope which are his celebrations of the Lord's Supper; over a lifetime such services play their part in etching hope into his consciousness. But they will be able to play that part only if he also dwells on his hope in the difficult circumstances of the daily struggle, only if his hope has been secularized and toughened by reflection on the hopelessness of all those earthly hopes which beckon so alluringly to his heart.

❊ 8 ❊
Compassion

ONE of the most terrible things about dying, as Ivan Ilych
experienced it, was that his family and friends made him feel so
utterly alone in it. They were in the bloom of health and pleasure, in the midst of social hilarity and vigorous activity. He, in
his disgusting misery, weakness, and despair, was an alien to
them. There was only one person who took a different attitude:

> He saw that no one felt for him, because no one even
> wished to grasp his position. Only Gerasim recognized
> it and pitied him. And so Ivan Ilych felt at ease only
> with him. He felt comforted when Gerasim supported
> his legs (sometimes all night long) and refused to go to
> bed, saying: "Don't you worry, Ivan Ilych. I'll get sleep
> enough later on," or when he suddenly became familiar
> and exclaimed: "If you weren't sick it would be another
> matter, but as it is, why should I grudge a little trouble?"
> Gerasim alone did not lie; everything showed that he
> alone understood the facts of the case and did not con-
> sider it necessary to disguise them, but simply felt sorry
> for his emaciated and enfeebled master. Once when
> Ivan Ilych was sending him away he even said straight
> out: "We shall all of us die, so why should I grudge a
> little trouble?"—expressing the fact that he did not think
> his work burdensome, because he was doing it for a
> dying man and hoped someone would do the same for
> him when his time came. (*The Death of Ivan Ilych and
> Other Stories*, p. 138)

Compassion is the construal of a suffering or deficient person as a cherished fellow. Like other emotions, it is not a dis-
interested construal. The terms of the fellowship—the suffering
or deficiency—determine a self-concern (I care about my sufferings and deficiencies), and the construal of the other as a
fellow in these terms thus shapes and motivates a concern for
him. Compassion is a form of love, but distinguishable from

other forms of love by the terms of its fellowship. Friendship, family affection, spousely love, and love for fellow believers all differ from compassion in that the terms of this latter fellowship are suffering or deficiency: the beloved (why not use that word?) is viewed in terms of a fellow-suffering (actual or potential) or a fellow-deficiency. When I perceive someone compassionately, the weakness or suffering or sin I see in him is a quality I see also in myself. Of course I can have compassion for someone I love as a friend, a family member, a spouse, or a believer; my point is just that compassion is not the same as these other forms of love, and that the difference lies in how the beloved is viewed.

From the fact that compassion is a form of love based in the fellowship of suffering and deficiency, it follows that it is a form of *neighbor*-love. By "neighbor" the Christian means anybody we come in contact with. Not just anybody is my friend, a member of my family, my spouse, or a fellow Christian. These bonds of fellowship are limited by qualifications that not everybody has or can have, and so they are not forms of neighbor-love. But a vulnerability to suffering, weakness, and death and a participation in sin are things I have in common with absolutely every human being, and a fellowship based on this feature is one I can have with anybody who comes along. Gerasim's willingness to devote so much of himself to Ivan Ilych is not the result of any special tie of family or friendship; he simply sees another mortal, like himself, in need. And in this vision of community his heart goes out. And then his shoulders.

There are sentimental people whose hearts seem to go out to the suffering while their legs and arms and shoulders remain inert. But where compassion is strong enough to be called a character trait, it typically results in an *action* congruent with viewing the other as a sufferer much like oneself. If the suffering is physical or mental, the action will probably be some effort to alleviate it. If it is a deficiency, such as some weakness of will, body, or mind, forbearance is often in order. If the deficiency is ethical, compassion will typically move to forgiveness, gentleness, and mercy, with the indescribably many forms of behavior typical of these. I too am susceptible to the suffering I see in this other, I too am weak and deficient in many ways, I too will soon die, I too am a sinner in need of forgiveness—when these considerations issue in helpfulness, patience, mercy, and gentleness, then compassion has prevailed.

THE vice corresponding to compassion can be called "aloofness." It is the disinclination to see the commonality between myself and the sufferer I meet, the inclination to dwell on differences between myself and the deficient one—differences which create a distance between him and me. Aloofness is either a matter of denying an obvious similarity between myself and another or of accepting the appearance of difference between myself and some deficient person.

The Pharisee who prays "I thank thee God that I am not like that publican" accepts the appearance of his own righteousness and the appearance of sinfulness in the publican and misses the commonality. After all, it is *well known* what a despicable thing it is to take money from one's own people for the maintenance of the foreign occupation. And as for himself, it is clear for all to see that he is fastidious in meeting his religious obligations. The Pharisee is the willing victim of standardized, unspiritual, public ways of seeing: being spiritually blind to himself, he cannot see others as they really are. And thus an illusion of distance is created: because he does not know himself, others look so very different to him. But why does he not know himself? Because in an important sense he has not become serious about his standing before God—he has not passionately undertaken the project of becoming inwardly fit for the kingdom, pure in heart before the Father who sees in secret. He is a nice person with a conveniently external moral standard, who does not *want* to apply any other standard. He has undertaken the task of becoming pure in action, but not that of becoming ethically good. Were he to undertake this most deeply human of projects, he would soon see that even this supercilious attitude toward the publican was enough to render him roughly equal to them in moral status. (Jesus seems to imply that whatever difference might be left would not be to the Pharisee's advantage.) And with this awareness of his own failure of the heart, he could begin to take that gentle, nurturing attitude toward publicans and prostitutes that we have been calling compassion.

The aloofness of the Pharisee is shocking and proverbial, of course, and he is hardly lacking in fellow travelers. We all know, and are or have been, such moral oafs and nincompoops: "No, I must say, I make it a policy not to visit hospitals. It is just too depressing, all those people lying in beds, sick and hurt, with the smell of disinfectant and medicine (and sometimes even worse things) in the air. Of course I feel sorry for them, but I just can't take it. And for the past ten years I've made it a strict policy not to go to funerals. I've found that when I do go, I wake with bad dreams and terror in the middle of the night; I guess I'm just a sensitive soul, but I find it even spoils my bridge sometimes, and I get to drinking more, which is such a distressing thing. My daughter has fallen in with a bunch of hippies that meet in an old store building in the rough section of town, where they sing hymns and feed the bums and try to get jobs for teenagers. It's a sweet thought, but completely unrealistic; and I have to admit it strikes me as a little bit *indecent,* for a nice girl like my Judy. Those people are so *different*, and so unpredictable. As for me, when I drive through that section of town, I keep the windows rolled up tight.

Ivan Ilych's family and the Pharisee and the nice upper middle class lady whose heart I just bared to you are the sort of people who dismay us Christians. Indignation is what we feel, indignation on behalf of injured humanity. *They* probably think that prostitutes and dope addicts and bums and people on welfare are the ones that are going to hell, and quite naturally too, if you conceive of hell as a kind of trash barrel. But we, being radical Christians (or at least sort of radical—we read *Sojourners* and think it's the greatest thing to come down the pike since Dorothy Day), have a deeper insight. We know what real trash looks like. And it ain't prostitutes and welfare recipients.

But even to us cognoscenti there perhaps cleaves a remnant of aloofness in the form of a stubborn stain. A young pastor glances at the clock and sees that he must put down a moving and fascinating article on St. Francis of Assisi that has appeared in the December issue of *Sojourners.* It is time to make the hospital rounds. He leaves the plush office provided by his affluent congregation and goes down and cranks up his symbolic 1962 Volkswagen. Everything goes well as he visits a young wife who has just delivered a healthy girl baby and a teenager who broke his leg in football practice. But the last visit of the day is more difficult: a fifty-year-old woman dying of lung cancer. He wants very much to be a good pastor and to sympathize with her and thinks to himself in the midst of the visit that he is not doing too badly. She seems to be deriving comfort from the visit, and he hasn't made any obvious blunders so far. The patient, shriveled and unable to leave the bed, asks him to lift her head and put a couple more pillows under it. As he does so, the muscles which fill his shirt strain against his sport jacket. Then he says a moving prayer with her and leaves. As he walks out into the balmy air of a spring evening in the city, he can't resist a certain sense of exaltation at being away from the hospital room and out among his own kind once more. What an alien being that sufferer seemed, lying so weak and helpless at death's door! He glances at his watch, and is glad to see that he has time to stop at the office on his way home, and finish that article on St. Francis.

Y OUNG people are not, in general, very compassionate. Even the nicest of high school students may think that treating a "nerd" as a fellow human being is inconceivably beyond the call of duty—roughly analogous to respecting the rights of cockroaches to hospitable treatment in one's home. Nerds, homosexuals, cripples, people over twenty-one, and other sufferers are occasions for hilarious (and almost innocent) jokes rather than objects of human concern. One obvious reason for this character deficiency in young people is that they have not suffered enough to identify readily with sufferers. Because of narrow experience, their hearts do not go out to people who are "different," but remain enclosed within their own skins. It is not that they fail to recognize that the other is suffering or deficient: indeed their jokes at his expense presuppose that they do. What they lack is a recognition of *themselves* in that suffering, a visceral impression of the connection between themselves (*their* weakness, vulnerability, sinfulness) and the suffering or deficiency of the other.

But merely having suffered does not guarantee compassion. Some who have suffered deeply become embittered about life or consumed with the project of self-protection. Compassion means that one's heart goes out to someone else, but people sometimes respond to suffering by turning their heart inward. Suffering becomes for them a reason for increased self-preoccupation, either in the form of efforts to get relief for themselves or to avoid a recurrence of their suffering or to indulge in self-pity over it. People learn different things from their trials: some selfishness, others compassion.

What makes the difference? How can a person turn his sufferings to his spiritual benefit and the blessing of others through compassion? A complete answer to this question would no doubt be very complicated, and perhaps no one knows or can know everything that goes into it; but a partial and rough answer does seem possible. Suffering can become the basis of compassion only if the person in some way comes to an *acceptance* of it. If I am always dissociating myself from my own death, sufferings, sins, and inadequacies — denying that they are "really" part of me and part of my condition in this life — then it is natural that I will keep my emotional distance from sufferers. If in my secret heart the answer to the question "Who am I?" is given entirely in terms of shining success, strength, health, pleasure, and being a good guy, then of course I am quite a different sort of being from these sufferers, these sinners, these unfortunate or even dying people. To be sure, I will have to acknowledge that they are human beings, and to that extent they bear an unsettling resemblance to myself; but it would be going too far to think of them as brothers and sisters, as fellows upon the road of human life. So if I refuse to accept my sufferings and deficiencies, no amount of them will make me a compassionate person.

For this reason the process of becoming transparent to one-self that we discussed in Chapter 3 is an important ground of compassion. That process forces me to come to terms with my vulnerability; I come to know viscerally and steadily that I am destined for death, and in one way or another I become reconciled to this fact. I get an emotionally clear view of myself in my darker aspect, and thus lay the groundwork for seeing as fellows those who are walking through the valley of the shadow of death. As I have suggested, this process is encouraged by the Christian hope. Those who believe that death is not the last word have a resource for facing death honestly which nonbelievers lack. So Christian hope is a psychological aid to compassion.

The compassion of the youth Gerasim, Tolstoy seems to be

telling us, is grounded in Gerasim's peasant (Christian) acceptance of his own vulnerability and transience. Because he is
relatively at peace about the prospect of his own death and about
the prospect of his undergoing the humiliating process of bodily
degeneration, he is able to be a genuine companion to the stink-
ing and groaning Ivan Ilych. By contrast, for the self-opaque
members of Ivan Ilych's family the latter's suffering is nothing
but a rather disgusting intrusion into their life, a nasty incon-
venience to be avoided if possible, and certainly nothing that
suggests an essential kinship with themselves.

W E have seen that the *experience* of suffering, finitude, and
sin is needed in the development of compassion; in addition,
one needs an *acceptance* of these as a part of one's identity. But
there are cases in which a person has experienced weakness,
and in some sense accepts that fact, and yet is not compassionate. An examination of such a case will help us to see a little
more deeply what we must mean by "acceptance." For not just
any sort of acceptance will do; what is required is that the individual accept his vulnerability as part of his *present* self.

The early chapters of Gordon Liddy's autobiography *Will*
recount the extreme measures he takes as a boy to overcome his
excessive fears. In each case the cure takes the form of confronting the fear: afraid of rats, he eats one; afraid of electrical storms,
he lashes himself sixty feet up a seventy-five foot pin oak in the
midst of violent wind and lightning. He also overcomes his fear
of pain by suffering it. At one point, he takes the position of
catcher on the baseball team because it involves getting hit by
bats and big boys bound for home plate, and nobody else wants
the position. He reports that he would go back into the play
while still hurt, and "with a convert's zeal I became contemp-
tuous of anyone who didn't want to play hurt" (p. 28). Liddy
expresses a bit of condescension toward his youthful "convert's
zeal," but this story foreshadows the grown-up Liddy's attitude
toward weak and cowardly people. With the continuing zeal of
a convert, he holds them in contempt: I overcame my weakness
and fear, and they could too; but they don't, so they are scum.
He is like the rich man who, having made it out of a poverty-
stricken youth, does not use his first-hand knowledge of poverty
as a basis for sympathizing with the poor, but instead makes it

a ground for dissociating himself still further from them: I made it, and so could they; but the vermin won't work.

In a perfectly good sense of "know," Liddy knows what it's like to be weak and fearful. He has not forgotten it, as his vivid writing about these experiences shows. And in a perfectly good sense of "accept," he accepts this fact about himself: he is not at all trying to cover it up; indeed, he is glorying in it, and glorying in revealing it to others. And yet his aloofness toward cowardly and weak people is especially virulent: he is not just indifferent to their plight, but positively hateful toward them on account of it. I suggest that this violent dissociation of himself from the weak and fearful is possible only because he does not identify his *present* self with the self he was when he was weak and fearful. He has contempt not only for others with these traits, but also for himself—that is, for the person he once was. There is obviously *some* sense in which he is the same person who was once weak and fearful, but emotionally he does not look upon that boy as being himself; he does not "identify" with him. Since he dissociates himself from himself insofar as he is weak, his "self-knowledge" does not become the ground for appreciating the commonality between himself and those others. And note the propriety of the quotation marks I just put around "self-knowledge": in one perfectly good sense, this is not *self*-knowledge. For what Liddy knows in remembering the boy he was before his courageous acts is an alien self, a self he no longer owns to be himself, a self he has rejected.

Liddy is unwilling to identify with the cowardly boy he once was for a number of reasons. His upbringing seems to have predisposed an obsession with strength, and his entire autobiography confirms that he is so obsessed. His passion for being personally strong is not balanced by other passions which might mitigate his fear of weakness. Second, his book implies that Liddy is still suffering from a certain lack of self-confidence, that he still needs to "prove" himself; and he proves himself again and again by being a tough guy. (I am not saying he's any less confident than most of us.) If Liddy were cooler about himself, just a little less afraid of being caught with his pants down (that is, if he had more of the deep liking of himself that I talked about in Chapter 5), he might find it in his heart to reach out to that fearful boy who grew up in the '30s—and hug him emotionally to himself. And that would be the beginning of a new attitude to others who are weak and fearful. Third, having given up Catholicism, Liddy perhaps has no conceptual framework pressing him to understand himself in any other way than as the self which he obviously seems presently to be—a man in the strength of maturity with certain mental, emotional, and physical powers.

It doesn't seem to me that Liddy can be faulted epistemically for dissociating himself from the weak person he once was and the weak person he will someday again become (if he lives long enough). It is not as though he has *forgotten* what he once was or has *failed to reckon* with what he will probably sometime be. Nor is one under any logical compulsion, having noted the normal career of the human organism from weakness to strength to weakness again, to identify one's present self with all stages in that career. It may seem to us a little narrow-minded of him, and maybe psychologically imprudent (see Chapter 3), to refuse to admit as part of his personal identity those features which he once had and may someday again have but which at the present moment he has succeeded in chasing away; but he cannot be accused of being uninformed or absent-minded or illogical for doing so.

And so, it seems to me, there is an element of *choice* in self-knowledge at this point. We have to make some decisions about what we are going to accept as part of ourselves. Shall I accept as part of me the self that was crude and cruel at the age of fourteen? That was weak and cowardly at the age of ten? Or shall I deny that earlier self, identifying myself narrowly in terms of the traits I presently possess? Shall I accept as part of me the condition I may one day be in—of poverty, disease, weakness, senility—or shall I accept only what I more or less obviously now am? And when it comes to looking at others, the question will be, Shall I see in a weak and cowardly person, or an old confused person, or a crude and arrogant person, a fellow human, dear to me? Or shall I see in such a person a member of a different class than mine, a class I did or will, admittedly, belong to, but which I do not accept as part of my present self?

THE Christian is under pressure to stretch her self-concept rather than shrink or restrict it. She is encouraged to pick up analogs of weakness in her past and possible future as well as her present and, using these as points of departure, to see commonalities between herself and her weak neighbor. She is under the pressure of God's love to include in her self-understanding many features which to a prosaic, empiricist, and unspiritual eye would seem obvious candidates for exclusion. In the bloom of health she can identify with the sick and dying. In the strength of her maturity the weakness of a child does not seem alien to her. In the fullness of sainthood she can see herself in a criminal who has committed the most outrageous crimes. In the gentleness of her own humility she can "relate to" the rough arrogance and self-righteousness of a ruthless, money-grubbing member of the Moral Majority. All this may seem paradoxical and impossible to the non-Christian. But to the Christian it is the glory of her life, the imperative imitation of God.

For the Christian story is that of Emmanuel, God with us. In it God is not just near us, or beside us; he is even closer than that, for he is *one* of us. It is the story of his "identifying" with us in the most literal sense—of his altering his identity in our direction and for our sakes. He did not just sympathize with us from a close proximity, stand beside our hospital bed as it were. He took on human nature, including bodiliness, susceptibility to pain and death, the whole range of human sadness and joy, and even, mysteriously, sin. Paul exhorts the Christians at Philippi to imitate God's compassionate "seeing": "Have this mind among yourselves, which you have in Christ Jesus, who, though he was in the form of God, did not count equality with God a thing to be grasped, but emptied himself, taking the form of a servant, being born in the likeness of men" (Phil. 2:5–7). And to the Corinthian church Paul writes, "for our sake he made him to be sin who knew no sin, so that in him we might become the righteousness of God" (2 Cor. 5:21). In Jesus, God the Son chooses to extend his identity to encompass our condition. God is "broadminded," even about sin. He spreads his mind as a hen spreads her wings to cover every last chick, down to the weakest and most obstreperous in her brood. But he is not like silly people who are sometimes called broadminded, when in fact they are only characterless—weakminded, weakhearted, passionless, and morally confused. In such people broadmindedness about sin is just a deficiency of concern about sin and its consequences. God's broadmindedness means that, however much he abhors sin, he is willing not to dissociate himself from us, even on this account—indeed, he takes the initiative in associating himself with us as closely as possible, precisely on this account. In God's compassion the Christian has the warrant and charge to go and do likewise.

In the first four sections of this chapter I have spoken of human compassion as recognizing in someone else's lowliness an analog of the same lowliness that I can find, at least potentially, in myself. But ideologically narrowminded people like Gordon Liddy raise for us the question about how far I must go in drawing into my self-understanding features of human beings which are not actually *my* features *now*. I have admitted that a reasonable person is not compelled by either the facts or logic to understand herself in such a way that she sees others compassionately. We are confronted here with a choice. Non-Christians who are compassionate, and indeed most Christians who have not received explicit teaching on this matter, make such choices without much reflection. They make them "instinctively." They do what comes naturally. And what comes naturally is choosing to understand ourselves in such a way that we have a certain degree of compassion for others. The philosopher David Hume even held that "sympathy" is a universal human trait. Though this opinion does not seem to be borne out by the facts, and people vary greatly in the amount of sympathy they have for one another, it is surely true that there are tendencies in the human breast to identify with others when they are suffering, and the upbringing of many people makes them at least somewhat more broadminded than Gordon Liddy.

But the absolute center of the Christian faith, the model for all Christian seeing and behaving, is the compassionate incarnation of God in Jesus Christ. The idea of a narrowminded Christian is a contradiction. Broadmindedness is a conscious choice, but for the Christian the choice has already been made; to accept God's mercy in Jesus is to place oneself under constraint to strive for a broadness in one's self-concept and in one's mercy. When a person comes to acknowledge that Jesus is the Lord, she no longer has any choice about how far to go in identifying herself with weak, suffering, or sinful people. Because there is no person too lowly for her Lord, there is none too lowly for

her either. For this reason the Christian community does not
settle for whatever compassion comes naturally, but educates
for it. It holds constantly before itself the tender stooping love
of God and by so doing constantly seeks to stretch the self-
concepts of its individual members into a broadmindedness imitative of its Lord's.

From the Christian point of view, only God *chooses* to identify with the weak and sinful. For in his case he who was not
weak and not sinful *became* weak and *became* like a sinner for
the sake of the weak and sinful. But in compassion the Christian
does not become weak and sinful for the sake of some fellow
human being; instead she acknowledges a commonality between
herself and this sufferer, a commonality of which there is abun-
dant evidence for anyone who has eyes to see. For a sinner to
be Christianly merciful is not for her to be first a judge, honorable and wise and just, and then secondly to stoop in generous
condescension to pronounce a milder sentence than the sinner
deserves, or even to let him off scot free. No, Christians do not
stoop when they are compassionate; only God stoops. To be
merciful as a Christian is not in any way to be merciful as a
judge (even if by some social necessity a Christian happens to
be cast in the role of judge). It is, instead, to see that sinner
as a fellow sinner. And in the face of the moral hierarchies
suggested to us by human standards of discrimination, by the
differences so obvious between us upright citizens and the
murderers, rapists, thieves, and cheats who fill our prisons, it
is an ongoing task of Christian education to keep ourselves aware
of our full membership in the universal brotherhood of
miscreants.

THE story of God's incarnation provides a model of compassion for the Christian to imitate and an imperative for him to
do so. But the gospel is not just a model and imperative, but
also, and primarily, good *news*. It is the news of our redemption
from sin and death, information about a new status, hitherto
unknown to us, that we enjoy before God. It is the declaration
that we have been washed clean and are destined to live in his
eternal kingdom. The accomplishment of this new status is
closely, though mysteriously, tied up with God's humbling himself and identifying with us in the life, but especially in the death,

of Jesus of Nazareth. I want now to say a little about how believing this declaration engenders compassion. And I shall do
this by relating compassion to the other two fruits of the Spirit
that I have discussed, gratitude and hope.

If I believe the gospel in a spiritual way (that is, if I passionately construe my life in its terms), then I see myself very
gladly as the recipient of this undeserved gift of eternal life, and
I see God as my absolute benefactor. This is Christian gratitude,
and it has two consequences relevant to compassion: a sense of
absolute dependency and a sense of blessing.

The "earning mentality" that is so often the basis of aloofness is eradicated to the extent that a person is Christianly grateful. If I know myself to be absolutely dependent on God for the
most important thing in life, then any accomplishments I may
have to my credit are swamped in this undergirding common
dependency, and so are prevented from becoming the basis for
dissociating myself from those who are weak or needy or sinful.
In this manner, Christian gratitude clears the way for that sense
of identification with others which is so basic to compassion.

But Christian gratitude is much more than a sense of absolute dependency. That by itself would not motivate compassion. If I am grateful to God in Jesus Christ, I see myself as
perfectly and radically blessed, as accepted and important in the
universe, as one on whom God's love has been showered, as a
worthy one. Perfect Christian gratitude is not just a sense of
absolute dependency, but also a sense of spiritual well-being. It
unites being humbled with being exalted. So gratitude involves
the self-confidence which is also necessary to compassion. To be
grateful is to have the self-possession to be unselfish, to be sufficiently secure at the center to be unself-centered. Gratitude is
the *glad* acceptance of my status as beneficiary of God's grace;
it is the self-accepting acceptance of God's gift; it is the healthy
being-at-one with myself as poor and weak and unworthy. And
so genuine gratitude to God practically guarantees compassion.
To the person who is filled with thankfulness to God in Jesus
Christ, compassion is not a duty to which he forces himself more
or less against his will; being outgoing, self-giving, is "the most
natural thing in the world."

Christian hope is the construal of our future as life without
death in a state of perfect obedience to God and perfect fellow-

ship with all others. Like gratitude, it predisposes or enables compassion in at least two ways. First, it can dispel a basic cause of our faltering in compassion. When a person we are trying to help is obtuse to our graces or makes no progress, we may lose enthusiasm and tend to go our own more selfish way, thinking the situation hopeless. And indeed, the situation may be hopeless, from the heathen standpoint. There may be little or no hope, by worldly ways of reckoning, for a person with a certain disease, or mutilated by a perverse upbringing, or deficient mentally. And sin seems so intractable. Furthermore, from the purely secular standpoint there isn't any ultimate hope for any of us. As Bertrand Russell declares, ". . . that no fire, no heroism, no intensity of thought and feeling, can preserve an individual life beyond the grave; that all the labours of the ages, all the devotion, all the inspiration, all the noonday brightness of human genius, are destined to extinction in the vast death of the solar system" (*Mysticism and Logic,* p. 51) is a fact which must underlie our entire outlook on ourselves and others, if we are lucid secularists. It is almost a tautology that hopelessness, whether particularized or cosmic, tends to discourage. What is the use of going on, if in the end I will inevitably be foiled? If all is vanity, why should I bother with the unnatural project of identifying with the poor and weak when I am rich and strong? Why should I not accept the advice of Qoheleth, that "there is nothing better for a man than that he should eat and drink and find enjoyment in his toil" (Eccl. 2:24)? But in hope the Christian dares to believe that the things he does in imitation of Jesus are not destined to be foiled. Much of human endeavor will be brought to nothing, but these imitative acts will count; they will somehow be taken up and preserved in the kingdom. And so in the face of the many appearances that discourage compassion, the Christian's hope is a source of strength.

But not only does Christian hope defend our compassion against the discouragement of hopelessness; there is, secondly, something about the *thing* Christians hope for that presses us toward compassion. We hope for the kingdom of God, the kingdom which began to break in upon the world in the life and death of Jesus. In other words, we hope for a social condition in which our own identification with one another will reflect the Son of God's identification with each of us. A sharp example of the way the Christian vision of the kingdom determines compassion is found in Malcolm Muggeridge's book on Mother Teresa of Calcutta, *Something Beautiful for God*:

> Accompanying Mother Teresa, as we did, to these different activities for the purpose of filming them — to the Home for the Dying, to the lepers and unwanted children, I found I went through three phases. The first was horror mixed with pity, the second compassion pure and simple, and the third, reaching far beyond compassion, something I had never experienced before — an awareness that these dying and derelict men and women, these lepers with stumps instead of hands, these unwanted children, were not pitiable, repulsive or forlorn, but rather dear and delightful; as it might be, friends of long standing, brothers and sisters. How is it to be explained, the very heart and mystery of the Christian faith? To soothe those battered old heads, to grasp those poor stumps, to take in one's arms those children consigned to dustbins, because it is his head, as they are his stumps and his children, of whom he said that whosoever received one such child in his name received Him. (p. 38)

Jesus called himself the light of the world, and this incident is a vivid instance of his shedding light. The third phase of Muggeridge's consciousness of the people to whom Teresa was ministering is obviously what I have been calling compassion: in these weak and suffering ones, Muggeridge sees "dear and delightful . . . friends of long standing, brother and sisters." But he sees them as his brothers and sisters because he sees them as ones whom Christ first identified with, owning them as *his* brothers and sisters. Indeed, Christ's identification with ones like these was so complete that he could say that whoever received one of these in his name received *himself*. So Jesus is the light which shines upon these derelicts and lepers and unwanted children and reveals, to those who have eyes to see, that they are dear brothers and sisters, fellow members of the kingdom of God. And this is Christian compassion.

There is something else worth mentioning in this connection, and that is that Jesus called not only himself but also his *disciples* the light of the world. And I daresay Teresa was in fact functioning as such a light to the eyes of Muggeridge that day.

It might be that he would never have seen those people objectively, would never have gotten beyond his "horror mixed with pity" and his "compassion pure and simple," had he not been *introduced* to them by that holy woman. She is a derivative light for lighting up blind eyes and letting them see with compassion—derivative from her Lord. But she is like him in this respect: just as he created, by his compassion, a miniature and a foretaste of his kingdom on the hills and in the towns of Galilee and Judea, so she has created a miniature and foretaste of it in the heart of Calcutta. The vision which the two of them allow, along with all his other compassionate disciples across the ages, is a vision determined by that thing for which Christians hope, the fellowship of the kingdom of God.

I have said that the third phase of Muggeridge's consciousness is a good example of Christian compassion. And yet he himself refuses this name for it, saying that it reaches "far beyond compassion." Why does he think "compassion" a name not worthy of this holy emotion?

One reason, I think, is that the word (along with the near equivalents "pity" and "sympathy") has acquired a negative connotation. The word popularly no longer refers to the state of mind and heart in which an individual sees a sufferer as a genuine fellow. It seems to refer, instead, to an attitude that is somewhat aloof, condescending, and patronizing. Thus an effective way to insult somebody nowadays is to say "I pity you" or to look at him pityingly.

Another reason for not endorsing compassion "pure and simple" might be the feeling that it tends to be a mere sentiment, a property of somewhat flighty and hysterical people. Ethical character, it will be said, does not belong to scatterbrains; it is made of tougher stuff than compassion. Some people are so "sensitive," so strongly "moved" by the sight of other people's suffering, that they are discombobulated by it. Confronted with it they cannot think, and have little inclination (and little psychological ability) to help.

Such people may get a reputation, among the undiscerning, for being deeply compassionate; after all, they are so much more moved by suffering than ordinary people are. But it is clear that these are not really compassionate people, any more than are the people who faint at the sight of blood. I suspect that in beholding the other's sufferings, which are so upsetting to him, such a man does not much empathize with a real *other* person. Instead, the other's sufferings are perhaps for him a kind of window through which shines the frightfulness of his *own* existence. And indeed, it is in many cases an irrationally exaggerated frightfulness. (Maybe he would be *less* disconcerted by this suffering if it were his own, because when it is his own, reality checks his imagination.) What such a person lacks is a kind of presence of mind, an assimilation of experience of suffering, a mature resignation and measured judgment about it, a deep courage and self-control, an encompassing self-confidence in the face of the darker possibilities of existence. He who is Christianly compassionate, able to see himself in this sufferer and thus to see the sufferer as a dear fellow human, is able to do this because he himself is personally strong in these ways. Neal Plantinga has likened Christian compassion to soft, tough leather; you wouldn't want a baseball glove made either of tissue paper or of steel. And so it is with compassion: it's no good if it's so tender that it falls apart when it's smacked with reality, but it's also no good if it's so hard that reality just bounces off. And that's the way Christians are when they're grown up: compassion makes them both soft and tough, both vulnerable and stable.

COMPASSION is directed primarily at people who are in some obvious trouble. But I want to say a word or two about the relevance of compassion to people who to all appearances are "winners." Such people, especially if they are arrogant or ruthless, may not seem fit objects of compassion. And yet they very often (always?) are. Sometimes the most powerful and crass person is really a sufferer, a lonely one, a frightened one. It takes resoluteness and a bit of empathetic insight to see through the facade of strength and boasting and arrogance and wealth and power and intelligence and to see, as it were, a precious little one in trouble, a child of God, one of his lost, beloved sheep.

I know a man whose pastor was such a person. On the surface he ruled the church with an iron hand, used "political" tactics to consolidate and perpetuate the power of his position, and reserved his attention for the rich and powerful people in the congregation. He centered his "ministry" on things that showed to the lust of the eyes and the pride of life, such as thick new carpets and curtains for the parlor, perpetual paint jobs throughout the building, landscaping, and a smooth and sumptuous Sunday morning service. He tended to undercut the position of his colleagues on the church staff, and not to communicate with them. He obviously knew what the gospel was, because he persuasively included it in five or six sermons during his seven-year tenure in the church. But in retrospect one suspected that those were calculated occasions, the last one being the morning on which the pastoral search committee from a plush church on the west coast was visiting. To the relief of the more discerning members of the congregation, that committee took the bait.

My acquaintance had a stormy relationship with this man during his pastorate. An especially difficult episode occurred when the Consistory was sponsoring the purchase of a rather expensive wooden fence to protect the churchyard from unwelcome feet. In a meeting he raised an objection to this use of the Lord's money, and was told by the pastor that the proper channel for such an objection was a letter to the Consistory. As he wrote the letter, it bore down on him that the fence folly was not isolated, but was the result of the church's not being given spiritual leadership. So he decided to surround the fence with its spiritual context by including in the letter an analytical critique of two or three of the pastor's recent sermons, and challenging the members of the Consistory to require the pastor to teach Christian discipleship, thus warding off future fence follies. When the pastor had recommended a letter to the Consistory, this was not what he had in mind.

When the letter was read before the elders at the next meeting of the Consistory, the pastor was furious and dismayed. His hand was being called before the very people whose trust and respect he most needed. When my acquaintance got wind of how much the pastor felt personally injured by the letter, he called him up and apologized, as far as he could, and sought reconciliation. The reconciliation was at best grudging and distrustful, but it did mean that the two men saw one another more frequently than hitherto. For a few Sundays after the letter, the sermons seemed to have a bit more Christian content, but the effect did not last long, and on the whole the letter seemed only to have made the pastor still more self-protective and ruthless in his methods.

My acquaintance admits that in his naivete he was surprised to see that the letter caused the pastor such a sense of personal injury. The man had appeared to him a tough guy who could take anything, a dapper sophisticate in command of the situation, clear about what he wanted and ruthless in his approach to getting it. When it appeared how wrought up the man became, my acquaintance began to see him differently. Now he seemed to him almost like a confused child. Maybe he was desperately grasping after control of others because he felt so powerless and out of control of himself. Throughout his relationship with this pastor, my acquaintance vacillated between an angry view of him and a more compassionate one. Sometimes he wanted to do anything he could to run the pastor out of town, to get him to stop destroying the church and to punish him for what he had already done. But at times of more penetrating insight, his heart went out to him in the desire to nurture this lost soul. He found himself struggling to see more compassionately and very often, to his discredit, losing the struggle.

I am not saying there is never a time to be angry and hold a person responsible for his misdeeds. But usually behind those misdeeds is also a crippled person, one who needs not attacking, but help. And even if we decide, after due searching with the eyes of compassion, that strong opposition is called for, the strategy of the opposition will almost always be qualified by the compassion. In the case of my acquaintance, if he had had the insight of compassion from the beginning of his tangle with the pastor, he would probably not have written that letter, for he would have anticipated the hurt and hardening that it would cause. He might instead have tried to befriend the pastor, to *nurture* him toward reform rather than just blast him out of the saddle. There is almost no human situation to which some exercise of compassion is not appropriate; for to see with the eyes of compassion is to approach with gentleness and kindness, and these are never out of season. To be always poised to address weakness and suffering is the aggressive and creative compassion of the Christian. To search the situation compassionately (even if, in the unlikely event, one doesn't find any weakness in the offending person) is to soften and humanize one's approach, and probably to make it more effective in changing people for the good. For when it comes to improving people, love is stronger than anger, and nurture more effective than injury.

Before we end, we must ask how we can nurture compassion in ourselves. How can we become more spiritual, more prolific bearers of this fruit of the Spirit of our Lord Jesus Christ? The answers, it seems to me, divide into three groups: first, we must do those things that create in us a passion for the kingdom of God; second, we must act compassionately; and third, we must set our minds daily on the things of the Spirit.

All of the peculiarly Christian emotions are founded upon a passionate interest in the kingdom of God. We have seen this in Chapters 6 and 7 with respect to thanksgiving and hope. It seems to me that the relation of compassion to this fundamental Christian enthusiasm is somewhat less direct. When I give thanks in the most centrally Christian manner, I give thanks for the kingdom of God or for my inclusion in it. When I hope in the most centrally Christian manner, I hope for the kingdom of God. But when I am compassionate in the most centrally Christian manner, I am not compassionate toward the kingdom of God. Instead, I am compassionate toward a "neighbor," some individual or group of individuals with whom I have more or less directly to do. I model my compassion upon that act by which God established his kingdom (the incarnation); I am moved to compassion partly by my gratitude to God who has spared me for his kingdom; and in compassion I see my neighbor by the light of the kingdom, seeing him as one with whom Christ has compassionately identified himself. So compassion is tied in tightly with the gospel manner of construing the world, and takes root in the individual heart in ultimately the same way that the gospel does: by infusing the individual with a passionate concern for God's kingdom and for his or her participation in it. Thus a fundamental, though somewhat indirect, way of nurturing compassion is to undertake the disciplines described in Chapters 3 through 5.

The second kind of discipline for deepening compassion is action. Even if I do not "feel" very compassionate at a given moment, I may nevertheless be in a position to say a kind word, lend a hand, or make some gesture of solidarity. And if I do, there is a good chance that felt compassion will not be long in supervening. For my action tends to influence my construal of the other; in performing a gesture of solidarity with another I am likely to begin to *see* myself as in solidarity with him (especially if I am aware that he sees me as in solidarity with him). Also, such an action tends to draw me into practical fellowship with the other, and so to introduce me more intimately to his humanity and his troubles, thus giving me more vivid grounds for empathy. And third, if he in turn welcomes my action, this is likely to lure me into the fellowship (for after all, being a love among equals, compassion is ultimately and ideally a form of friendship) and thus to deepen my present compassion—not to mention the "positive reinforcement" it gives me for compassionate acts in general.

And finally, St. Paul says that "those who live according to the flesh set their *minds* on the things of the flesh, but those who live according to the Spirit set their *minds* on the things of the Spirit." And he says to the Philippians, "Finally, brethren, whatever is true, whatever is honorable, whatever is pure, whatever is lovely, whatever is gracious, if there is any excellence, if there is anything worthy of praise, *think* about these things" (Rom. 8:5; Phil. 4:8; my emphasis). Having the Christian virtues is at least partly a matter of what occupies a person's thoughts. If a person thinks salacious thoughts, she is to that extent a salacious person; if covetous thoughts, she is a covetous person; if generous thoughts, she is a generous person; if God-loving thoughts, she is a God-loving person. I have argued throughout this book that Christian spirituality is a way of construing or attending to or thinking about ourselves, our world, and God. If that is true, it is natural that one kind of spiritual discipline that has always had a place in Christianity is *meditation*: setting one's mind on the things of the Spirit.

But what are the things of the Spirit, and what does it mean to set one's mind on them? I do not think Paul is recommending that we dwell on "the doctrine of the third person of the Trinity." He is not urging us to become experts on pneumatology! The things of the Spirit are the things that belong to the Spirit of God, that evince his Spirit, and that are fruits of his Spirit. The most central "thing of the Spirit" is Jesus Christ himself. One who wishes to become more compassionate will do well to turn his thoughts very definitely for a time each day to the compassion of God in Jesus Christ. As meditation on God's grace begins to take root on him, his way of "looking at things" will gradually be transformed. Another kind of thing of the Spirit is the lives and actions and words of spiritual Christians. To read or hear about Mother Teresa or Francis of Assisi can be a powerful contribution to the formation of compassion in a Christian's heart. And even books like the present one (I like to believe), in which we think a bit analytically and methodically about the Christian virtues, can perhaps turn a person's mind to the things of the Spirit—for humility, gratitude, hope, compassion, and longing for the kingdom of God are surely also things of the Spirit.

This is meditation that one does in a quiet hour alone with the Bible or some other book or sitting in church. But there is another kind, without which meditation in this more usual sense would be of little avail, a meditation occurring in the midst of the activities and interactions of life. It is done not in the closet but in the street, the office, the factory, at the dinner table, the beach, the football game. I am driving to work in heavy traffic and make a blunder, infuriating the driver behind me. When he gets a chance, he screeches around me, honking his horn and making an obscene gesture. This circumstance does not lend itself to compassionate seeing, but it is an opportunity for such. And so I remind myself that Christ died for that man as he did for me, that he and I are fellows in our vulnerability and sin. The Christian, unless he is a perfect saint, will find that compassionate seeing requires vigilance and continued effort. It requires concerted acts of compassionate attention throughout the day, a stretching of one's self-conceptions, an aggressive searching for hints of commonality with other persons, an intentional use of the gospel as a visualizing framework.

It is a virtue in books that they, with the reflections between their covers, come to an end, and preferably before page two hundred. But it is not a virtue in a Christian that his spiritual reflections come to an end. To set one's mind on the Spirit is life and peace, and the Christian does not cease hungering for these when he turns the last page. So there is something fittingly symbolic about the incompleteness of books like the present one:

it would be a pity if the thoughts were considered results, or the last word of the book were taken to be the last word on the subject. I trust that no one will be tempted to that mistake by the present discourse. It is but a sketch, with many details and major items missing, a sort of schematic indication of the intersection of spirituality and human emotion. We have not talked about all the fruits of the Holy Spirit—not even about all the ones that are emotions. For example, we have said next to nothing about the very important Christian virtue of peace. But even more, we have only barely touched on another class of Christian virtues which are *not* emotions, the ones that I referred to at the beginning of Chapter 2 as "strengths": self-control, patience, steadfastness, forbearance, perseverance, courage, and others. These too are fruits of the Holy Spirit, and deserve the kind of reflection we have devoted to the emotions. Perhaps, God willing, at another time and in another volume just as incomplete as this one, I will have occasion to give them some careful thought.

List of Works Cited

Barfoot, Edith. *The Witness of Edith Barfoot,* ed. by Sir Basil Blackwell.· Oxford: Basil Blackwell, 1977.

Boswell, James. *The Life of Johnson,* ed. by Christopher Hibbert. New York: Penguin Books, 1979.

Carothers, Merlin. *Power in Praise.* Plainfield, N. J.: Logos International, 1972.

Dickens, Charles. *David Copperfield.* New York: Modern Library, 1900.

Herbert, R. T. *Paradox and Identity in Theology.* Ithaca, N. Y.: Cornell University Press, 1979.

Hilton, Walter. *The Stairway of Perfection,* trans. by M. L. Del Mastro. Garden City, N. Y.: Doubleday and Co., 1979.

James, William. *The Principles of Psychology,* 2 vols. New York: Dover Publications, 1950.

Jastrow, Joseph. *Fact and Fable in Psychology.* Boston: Houghton, Mifflin and Co., 1900.

Kant, Immanuel. *Foundations of the Metaphysics of Morals,* trans. by Lewis White Beck. Indianapolis: The Bobbs-Merrill Co., 1959.

Kierkegaard, Søren. *The Sickness Unto Death,* trans. by Howard and Edna Hong. Princeton, N. J.: Princeton University Press, 1980.

Lewis, C. S. *The Abolition of Man.* New York: The Macmillan Co., 1947.

_____. *The Great Divorce.* New York: The Macmillan Co., 1946.

_____. *Miracles.* New York: The Macmillan Co., 1947.

Liddy, G. Gordon. *Will: The Autobiography of G. Gordon Liddy.* New York: St. Martin's Press, 1980.

MacDougall, William. *Character and the Conduct of Life.* London: Methuen Publishers, 1927.

Moltmann, Jurgen. *Theology of Hope,* trans. by James W. Leitch. New York: Harper and Row, 1967.

Muggeridge, Malcolm. *Something Beautiful for God.* Garden City, N. Y.: Doubleday and Co., 1977.

Murdoch, Iris. *The Sovereignty of Good.* New York: Schocken Books, 1971.

Phillips, D. Z. *Death and Immortality.* London: Macmillan, 1970.

Roberts, Robert C. *Rudolf Bultmann's Theology.* Grand Rapids, Mich.: Wm. B. Eerdmans Publishing Co., 1976.

Rouse, W. H. D., translator. *Great Dialogues of Plato.* New York: The New American Library, 1956.

Russell, Bertrand. *Mysticism and Logic.* Harmondsworth, Middlesex: Penguin Books, 1953.

Tolstoy, Leo. *The Death of Ivan Ilych and Other Stories.* New York: The New American Library, 1960.

Whitman, Walt. *Leaves of Grass.* New York: Modern Library, 1940.

Wittgenstein, Ludwig *Tractatus Logico-Philosophicus,* trans. by D. F. Pears and B. F. McGuinness. London: Routledge and Kegan Paul, 1961.